THE COMPLETE GUIDE TO
Residential Letting

Tessa Shepperson

The Complete Guide to Residential Letting
by Tessa Shepperson

1st edition 2000
2nd edition 2002
3rd edition 2003
4th edition 2004
5th edition 2005
6th edition 2006
7th edition 2008
8th edition 2010
9th edition 2012
10th edition 2013
11th edition 2014
12th edition 2015

Lawpack Publishing Limited
76–89 Alscot Road
London SE1 3AW

www.lawpack.co.uk

The right of Tessa Shepperson to be identified as the author of this work has been asserted by her in accordance with the Copyright, Designs and Patents Act 1988.

ISBN: 9781910143292
ebook ISBN: 9781910143308

Exclusion of Liability and Disclaimer

Whilst every effort has been made to ensure that this Lawpack product provides accurate and expert guidance, it is impossible to predict all the circumstances in which it may be used. Accordingly, neither the publisher, authors, nor any barristers or solicitors who have assisted in the production of this Lawpack product and updated or refined it, or whose name is credited as having so assisted and updated or refined it, nor retailers, nor any other suppliers shall be liable to any person or entity with respect to any loss or damage caused or alleged to be caused as a result of the use of the information contained in or omitted from this Lawpack product.

For convenience (and for no other reason) 'him', 'he' and 'his' have been used throughout and should be read to include 'her', 'she' and 'her'.

Contents

Important facts

This book contains the information and instructions for landlords letting residential properties. This book can be read in relation to lettings in England & Wales and in Scotland; any differences in law are highlighted. It is not intended for use in Northern Ireland.

The information it contains has been carefully compiled from professional sources, but its accuracy is not guaranteed, as laws and regulations may change or be subject to differing interpretations. The English law is stated as at 1 November 2015.

Approved under Scottish law by Anthony Gold, Solicitors.

Neither this nor any other publication can take the place of a solicitor on important legal matters. As with any legal matter, common sense should determine whether you need the assistance of a solicitor rather than rely solely on the information and forms in this book.

We strongly urge you to consult a solicitor if:

- substantial amounts of money are involved;
- you do not understand the instructions or are uncertain how to complete and use a form correctly;
- what you want to do is not precisely covered by this book;
- trusts or business interests are involved.

About the author

Tessa Shepperson qualified as a solicitor in 1990, and for nearly 20 years ran her own law firm, TJ Shepperson, specialising in residential landlord and tenant law. In 2013, she closed this down to concentrate on her Landlord Law online service, www.landlordlaw.co.uk, and her training company, Easy Law Training, www.easylawtraining.com.

Tessa is also the author of *The Quick Guide to Taking in a Lodger*, also published by Lawpack. She lives in Norwich and is married with one son.

Introduction

Being a landlord is not as easy as it may appear. It involves a lot of work, yet the general perception of landlords is that they have an easy life getting 'money for nothing'. It is important that landlords realise the extent of the obligations that they are taking on and are aware of their legal responsibilities. Landlords are subject to a plethora of regulations that are regularly amended or added to. Usually they involve penalties for non-compliance. These regulations are intended to protect the tenant; however, they can also protect the landlord to a certain extent because if he complies with them he will have a good defence to any claims that may be made against him by the tenant. Also good quality properties are more likely to attract good quality tenants – the 'holy grail' of landlords. The landlord with a good tenant has far, far fewer problems than the landlord with a bad tenant.

This book is intended mainly to be a practical guide for new landlords of short-term residential tenancies, although it will, I hope, be useful to experienced landlords and may also be of interest to tenants. After some initial legal explanation, it aims first to guide you through the things that you should be considering before letting a property, and to help you through the process of getting the property ready for letting, finding a tenant, and making the agreement with the tenant. It then goes on to discuss what happens during a tenancy and what you can do if you have problem tenants. Finally, there is some discussion about what happens, or should happen, at the end of a tenancy.

This book is intended to be a general guide only. If you have any special or unusual problem, you should not rely solely on this book, but should seek independent legal advice. Up-to-date information can also be found on my website Landlord-Law Online, www.landlordlaw.co.uk, and on my Landlord Law Blog at www.landlordlawblog.co.uk.

Acknowledgements

It has been great fun writing this book, and my first thanks should go to my editor, Jamie Ross, for giving me the opportunity to write it.

Part of my research has been talking to landlords and to professionals in relevant fields. I am very grateful to all of them for giving up their time, and this book would not have been possible without them. Any remaining mistakes, however, are mine.

I am particularly indebted to Mike Stimpson and John Stather of the National Federation of Residential Landlords and to Nigel Stringer, all of whom kindly read the manuscript. My grateful thanks also go to all of the following (in no particular order): Colin Lawrence FCIH – Area Manager for Cambridgeshire, Suffolk & Norfolk Rent Service; Bruce Edgington, Solicitor – President, and David Brown FRICS MCIArb – Vice President, Chilterns, Thames & Eastern Rent Assessment Panel; David Bush FRICS – Bush Property Management Ltd; Malcolm Turton – Eastern Landlords Association and National Federation of Residential Landlords; Mike Edmunds – Housing Advisor, Norwich Advice Services; John Spencer – Principal Housing Improvement Officer, Norwich City Council; Paul E Carter – HM Principal Inspector of Health & Safety, Health & Safety Executive, Norwich; Beverley Whittaker – Benefits Manager, Revenue Service, Norwich City Council; David Beard and Jonathan Peddle – Norfolk Trading Standards; Robert Graver – Director, Alan Boswell Insurance Brokers Ltd; Nick Saffell FRICS – Partner, Brown & Co; Sally Baits – Solicitor, Norwich City Council; Ian MacLeod M.I.Fire.E – Fire Safety Officer, Norfolk Fire Service.

I am also indebted to all the various landlords I have known and acted for over the years, and to the landlords in the Eastern Landlords Association who have chatted to me at meetings about their problems and experiences as landlords. Many thanks also to my husband Graeme and my mother for their help and encouragement while I was writing this book.

Tessa Shepperson

CHAPTER 1

The legal framework

It is important that landlords understand the basic legal framework and the various types of lettings that exist. This is because these differences have important ramifications and implications for the rights of landlords and tenants. I will be discussing these in more detail later in the book.

Housing and the rights of tenants have always been important political issues and there has been a series of Acts of Parliament on housing matters over the years. This makes the whole subject legally rather complex. A landlord's or tenant's rights will, to a large extent, depend upon the Act of Parliament which regulates the tenancy, which in turn depends upon the date when the tenancy originally started. As this book is aimed at new landlords, I will primarily consider the legal situation for a new tenancy (as opposed to a new agreement for an existing tenancy) created after 1 October 2015. However, most of the general points discussed will still be very relevant for older tenancies and landlords with existing tenants. I will try to indicate in the text where any differences occur to assist landlords of older tenancies.

All landlords must keep informed of legal developments and changes in the law that they have to comply with. A lot of amendments came into force on 1 October 2015 under the Deregulation Act 2015. At the moment, the majority of these will only affect tenancies which were created new or which were renewed on or after 1 October 2015. However note that after 1 October 2018 they will apply to all ASTs.

To keep up to date with new developments follow the author's blog at www.landlordlawblog.co.uk, and/or subscribe to one of the many property journals such as *Property Investor News* or the *Landlord & Buy-*

to-Let Magazine, and/or join one of the landlord associations such as the National Landlords Association or the Residential Landlords Association.

Housing law in Wales: In 2014, the Housing (Wales) Act was passed which is due to bring in mandatory licensing and accreditation later in 2015, thus significantly differentiating the Welsh and English systems. The Renting Homes (Wales) Bill is also making its way through the Welsh Assembly and will bring further changes in due course. I will indicate in the text what changes are expected, as far as they are known at the time of writing.

Note

This book deals only with short-term lettings (i.e. for less than seven years). Long-term leases, normally purchased with a premium, are not covered.

Licences and tenancies

In landlord and tenant law generally, there is a fundamental difference between a licence and a tenancy. A licence is where the owner of the property gives someone permission to occupy it. A tenancy is where the tenant acquires a 'legal interest' in the property. This 'legal interest', i.e. the tenancy/lease, is more than just permission to live in the property for a while; it is something that is capable of being bought and sold, and can pass to another person after the initial tenant dies.

With a tenancy, one way of looking at it is to consider that the landlord 'sells' the property to the tenant for a period of time in exchange for rent and the right for the landlord to get the property back after the tenancy ends (what lawyers call the 'reversion'). So, in many respects, while the tenancy is in existence it is the tenant who 'owns' the property, not the landlord.

Property law being what it is, things are not as simple as that. The various Acts of Parliament which regulate short-term lettings have incorporated a number of rights and obligations into tenancies (and to a much lesser extent, licences) which the landlord is unable to exclude from the letting, however much he may want to (and even if the licensee/tenant agrees to them being excluded).

One of the most important rights that a tenant has is 'security of tenure'. This means that he can only be evicted from the property if the landlord follows the procedure laid down in the Act of Parliament which regulates that tenancy. In the 1980s, when the Rent Act 1977 applied to most tenancies, it was very difficult (and sometimes impossible) for landlords to evict tenants. Because of this, a landlord would sometimes try to claim that a letting was a licence so he could repossess his property through the courts. But in an important case in 1985, the courts ruled that whether an agreement is a tenancy or a licence depends upon the facts of the case and not what the agreement is called. For example, if the occupier has 'exclusive occupation' of all or part of the property and pays rent, then his occupation is normally deemed to be a tenancy, even if the document he signed is called a 'licence agreement'. However, if the occupier receives services (such as board and cleaning) as in bed-and-breakfast accommodation, then the occupation will usually be a licence.

There is little incentive nowadays for landlords to try to get round the legislation, as they have much greater rights under the Housing Acts 1988 and 1996, which apply to most new tenancies today (for Scotland, the Housing (Scotland) Act 1988 applies and Housing (Scotland) Act 2006). In particular, landlords can generally recover possession of their property through the courts, provided they follow the correct procedure. The legislation also implies various 'covenants' (i.e. legal obligations) into tenancies, the most important of which are the landlords' repairing covenants. These are considered further in the book, in particular in chapter 3.

Under the housing laws, tenancies will run on after any initial fixed term has expired (in the form of a new, 'periodic' tenancy) until they are ended in a recognised way. The most common ways for a tenancy to end are by what lawyers call 'surrender', i.e. if the tenant vacates/gives up possession of the property, or by the court making an order for possession. This is discussed in more detail in chapters 9 and 10. Some landlords mistakenly think that a tenancy ends when the fixed term ends and that if tenants stay on after this, they are 'squatters'. This is not the case; they still have a valid tenancy.

It is perhaps also worth mentioning that someone occupying a property under a tenancy, whether it is an assured shorthold tenancy (AST) in England & Wales, a short assured tenancy (SAT) in Scotland or a Rent Act tenancy, cannot acquire 'squatters rights' over the property, however long they stay there. The only situation where this could conceivably happen is where the tenant stops paying rent and has no contact whatsoever with the landlord for a period of more than 12 years. This is not going to happen very often!

As mentioned above, when a landlord grants a tenancy of a property to a tenant, he loses many of his rights over the property in exchange for the right to receive rent. This means that he loses the right to deal with or enter the property and can only do so with the permission of the tenant. This is the case even if you want to enter the property for a legitimate purpose, such as the quarterly inspection or the annual gas check. If the tenant forbids you to enter, any attempt to do so will be trespass (even though by forbidding you access the tenant may be in breach of his tenancy agreement). This remains the case even if the tenant is in arrears of rent. Many landlords find this hard to understand or accept and feel that as they own the property they have the right to come and go as they wish. This is not the case; by granting a tenancy you lose control over the property and this passes to the tenant. You will only recover the right to deal directly with the property again once the tenancy has ended.

Set out below are some of the most important types of tenancy and licence agreement that exist. In this book I primarily concentrate on ASTs. However, I have included comments on assured tenancies (ATs), Rent Act tenancies and licences where appropriate.

Tenancies

Assured tenancy (AT)

Almost all tenancies that are granted nowadays are assured tenancies. The tenant has exclusive occupation of all or part of the property and the landlord has the right to charge a market rent. The landlord's rights (or 'grounds') to repossess the property are as laid down in the Housing Act 1988 (in Scotland, the Housing (Scotland) Act 1988), the most important being to recover possession as of right if the tenant falls into rent arrears of more than two months (in Scotland, rent arrears of more than three months).

Assured shorthold tenancy (AST)

Assured shorthold tenancies are a type or sub-group of assured tenancy, where the landlord has the additional right to recover property at the end of the fixed term, the 'shorthold' ground, provided the proper notices have been served on the tenant. ASTs are the most common type of tenancy granted today, as most tenancies are now automatically ASTs unless the landlord specifies otherwise. In this book, unless otherwise stated, it is assumed that the tenancy under discussion is an AST.

Short assured tenancy (SAT) in Scotland

This is similar to an AST, but the tenancy agreement must specify that it is a SAT and the correct notice must be served, otherwise it is an assured tenancy.

Rent Act tenancies

If a tenancy was granted before 15 January 1989 (2 January 1989 in Scotland), it will be regulated by the Rent Act 1977 (or the Rent Act (Scotland) 1984). This Act was more favourable to tenants; for example, it is more difficult for the landlord to evict tenants, and he can normally only charge a 'fair rent'. Tenancies under the Rent Act can be either 'protected' or 'statutory', but for the purposes of this book I will refer to them all as Rent Act tenancies. As Rent Act tenancies are by their nature a shrinking category, less consideration will be given to them in this book. Note that you cannot convert a Rent Act tenancy to an AST by simply giving the tenant a new fixed-term agreement with Assured Shorthold Tenancy written at the top; whatever the agreement document states, the tenancy will remain a Rent Act tenancy.

Agricultural tenancies

Agricultural tenancies are not covered in this book.

Company lets

If a property is let to a company as opposed to an individual, then much of the current legislation which protects tenants' rights (e.g. in the Housing Acts 1988 and 1996) will not apply. In the past this was sometimes used as a device to prevent the tenant getting security of tenure. However, this is now no longer necessary. It is generally assumed in this book that the tenant will be an individual and not a company.

Lettings at a very high or a very low rent

If the rent is more than £100,000 per annum (this upper limit does not apply in Scotland) or less than £250 per annum (£1,000 per annum in Greater London), or less than £6 per week in Scotland, the tenancy is specifically excluded from statutory protection as set out in the Housing Act 1988 and the tenancy will by default be regulated under the 'common law', in the same way that tenancies with resident landlords are, as discussed below.

Before 1 October 2010 (1 December 2011 in Wales), the upper limit was £25,000. However as at that date, all tenancies with a rent of between £25,000 and £100,000 were automatically converted to assured shorthold tenancies.

Holiday lets

If a property is let for a bona fide holiday, normally for a period of weeks rather than months, the landlord can usually evict the occupiers if they refuse to leave, without getting a court order.

Rent-to-rent

This is a relatively new phenomenon that has gained in popularity. It is where a landlord lets his property to someone on the basis that he will arrange for the property to be sublet to tenants. The landlord is generally offered a guaranteed rent, and as it is the tenant who will be doing all the work in renting out the property, this arrangement can be very attractive.

However, you need to be very careful, as there have been a number of cases where dishonest tenants have cheated landlords, who have been left with damaged properties and no rent.

The system can work if it is set up properly, and there are some reputable rent-to-rent specialists. However, note that the tenancy agreement between you and your tenant cannot be an assured shorthold tenancy, as your tenant will not be living at the property himself. It will be a commercial tenancy. There may also be planning implications.

Licences

Lodgers

This is where someone lets a furnished room in his own home. The lodger has fewer rights (see below) and the landlord can evict him without getting a court order. Income up to a specified limit (currently £4,250 but rising to £7,500 from April 2016) is normally exempt from tax. For more information see *The Quick Guide to Taking in a Lodger*, written by Tessa Shepperson and also published by Lawpack.

Lettings which can be either a tenancy or a licence

Houses in multiple occupation (HMOs)

This is where a number of people occupy the same property but do not form a single 'household'. These can be tenancies; for example, where more than two unrelated people share a house or flat, or licences; for example, where homeless people are housed in bed-and-breakfast accommodation in a hostel.

Since the Housing Act 2004, which changed the definition of an HMO, came into force, many more properties will now be deemed HMOs which might not have been before.

Do note that the Housing Act 2004 does not apply in Scotland. Part 5 of the Housing (Scotland) Act 2006 provides for a licensing scheme for HMOs in Scotland, and that came into force in August 2011.

For more information on HMOs, see chapter 4.

Employees

If an employee is required to occupy accommodation for the purposes of his employment, then this will be a licence and not a tenancy. Otherwise, the accommodation will normally be a tenancy, provided of course that the other elements of a tenancy, as discussed above, apply.

Other

There are always exceptions to the rules. If there is something unusual about your property or the terms upon which you intend to let it, you should seek independent legal advice.

Note

This book does not cover tenancies where part of the premises are used for a business, e.g. a manager's flat in licensed premises.

Resident landlords

Where the owner of the property lives in the same building, a letting is generally excluded from the definition of an AT (or AST). But the resident landlord rules cannot apply if the landlord is a company, and the landlord must be occupying the property as his main home at the time the tenancy is granted. There are two types of resident landlord situation that now apply:

1. Where the landlord shares accommodation with a licensee (i.e. lodgers).

2. Where the tenant occupies self-contained accommodation in the same building, provided this is not a purpose-built block of flats (e.g. if the landlord has converted a large house into flats and lives in one of them). Here, a tenancy will be created but it will be regulated under the 'common law' and not the Housing Act 1988.

    In Scotland, the situation is different: a tenant who occupies self-contained accommodation in a converted house would automatically be on an AT. To fall outside the Housing (Scotland) Act 1988, the landlord must have some means of access through the tenant's accommodation or vice versa.

Resident landlords have the following legal advantages:

*   The tenant cannot refer the rent to the Residential Property Tribunal.

*   The minimum two-month notice period as for shortholds does not apply.

- Any damage deposit taken will not be subject to the tenancy deposit protection rules and will not have to be protected in one of the schemes.

- The protection from eviction legislation does not always apply (but see chapter 9).

- The statutory succession provisions do not apply (see below).

However:

- Resident landlords cannot use the accelerated possession procedure (see chapter 9) if they need to evict their tenants.

Note

If the landlord (or all of them if there is more than one) ceases to live at the property as his (or their) main home, the resident landlord exceptions will cease to apply.

New tenancies today

To summarise, as stated above, if a new tenancy is created, it will normally be an AST. This will happen automatically once the tenant gets into occupation, and a landlord cannot prevent a tenancy arising and avoid his legal obligations simply by failing to give a written agreement.

There are exceptions where an AST will not be created, and these are where there is a resident landlord or if the rent is very high or very low, or where the tenant is a limited company. In the private sector a new AT will normally only be created nowadays when a long (e.g. 99-year) lease comes to an end or when a family member 'inherits' a Rent Act tenancy. However they are very common in public sector housing (e.g. properties rented from Housing Associations).

In Scotland, a new tenancy created will only be a SAT if the correct form of tenancy agreement is used and an AT5 notice (see below) is served on the tenant prior to him signing the tenancy agreement. If the tenancy agreement is not properly drawn up as a SAT, the AT5 notice is not served or indeed if there is no written tenancy agreement, the tenancy will normally be an AT. A landlord cannot prevent a tenancy arising and avoid his legal obligations by failing to give a written agreement. If, in fact, the landlord does fail to give a written agreement rather than provide the tenant with a SAT, the tenant will then be entitled to additional rights and the landlord's ability to terminate the tenancy will be more limited.

Other legal matters landlords need to know

Fixed-term and periodic tenancies

Normally a tenancy agreement states that the tenancy is for a specific period of time (e.g. six months). This is known as a 'fixed-term tenancy'. However, once the fixed term comes to an end, this does not mean that the tenant has to leave. The Housing Act 1988 provides that immediately after the end of the fixed term, a new 'periodic' tenancy arises on the same terms and conditions as the preceding fixed-term tenancy, the 'period' to be based on how the rent was paid.

So, if the rent is paid monthly, it will be a monthly periodic tenancy; if paid weekly, it will be a weekly periodic tenancy; and if paid quarterly, it will be a quarterly periodic tenancy. The first period will start the day after the fixed term ends. Say this is Monday 1 January. If the tenancy is a weekly periodic one, the next period will start on Monday 8 January, and if it is a monthly one, the next period will start on 1 February, and so on. On the whole, it is advisable that the period should be either weekly or monthly. Periodic tenancies can continue indefinitely, until the landlord or tenant does something to bring the tenancy to an end.

In Scotland, once the fixed term comes to an end the tenancy will continue on the same terms and conditions as the fixed-term tenancy for the same period as the original tenancy agreement. So, if the original tenancy agreement was for six months, the tenancy will continue for a further six months.

Note that a tenant cannot turn into a 'squatter' if he stays on after his tenancy agreement has come to an end.

Section 20 notices

Before 28 February 1997, it was necessary to serve a special notice (called a 'Section 20 notice', because it was required by Section 20 of the Housing Act 1988) on a tenant, before a tenancy was created, if you wanted that tenancy to be an AST. This caused many problems for inexperienced landlords, as the notice had to contain certain prescribed information and was invalid if it did not. Once a tenancy had started, it was impossible for it to be converted into an AST if no Section 20 notice had been served or if the notice served was defective (although the courts have been prepared in some recent cases to overlook minor errors in Section 20 notices). Happily, Section 20 notices are no longer necessary for new tenancies, as they were made redundant by the Housing Act 1996, which came into force (so far as Section 20 notices were concerned) on 28 February 1997. Section 20 notices are still important, however, for tenancies created between 15 January 1989 and 27 February 1997. So if you are buying a property with sitting tenants, this is something you will need to check.

In Scotland, it is necessary to serve a notice called an AT5 on the tenant prior to entering into the tenancy agreement for it to be a SAT.

Guarantees

If a landlord is uncertain whether a tenant will be able to pay the rent, he can take security in the form of a guarantee. This is where someone else signs an agreement to confirm that he will pay the rent and any money due from the tenant, if the tenant defaults on his payments. For example, guarantees are normally taken from students' parents in student lets. If the student then leaves the property owing rent, the landlord can sue the guarantor for the student's rent arrears. A guarantee can either be included in the tenancy agreement itself, which the guarantor will sign as well as the tenants, or there can be a separate guarantee deed.

Note that if a new tenancy agreement is signed between the landlord and the tenant (particularly where there are changes, for example if the rent has been increased), a new form of guarantee should also be signed with the guarantor, as the old guarantee deed may no longer be valid.

Joint and several liability

Where more than one tenant has signed a tenancy agreement, then the general rule is that they will all be 'jointly and severally' liable for the rent.

For example, say four students (Matthew, Mark, Luke and John) are renting a house together and they all sign the same tenancy agreement for a total rent of £400 per month. They will no doubt have agreed between themselves that they will each pay £100 per month. However, if one of the four tenants, Mark, then stops paying his share (e.g. if he leaves the house), the landlord is entitled to claim the outstanding rent from any of the tenants, not just from Mark. The landlord is not bound by the tenants' own agreement to pay £100 each. So, if one of the tenants, say John, is wealthy, the landlord can sue just John and get a judgment against him for the outstanding rent, even though he has paid his share.

Also, if the landlord has taken a guarantee from the student's parents (as is often done in student lets), he can normally claim the whole of any outstanding rent from any one parent guarantor, as the parent will effectively be guaranteeing the whole of the rent, not just his son's share. This can be avoided to a certain extent by limiting the guarantor's liability, for example to a specified sum of money.

Letting your own home

If you have lived or are going to live in the property as your main residence, you have an additional mandatory ground for possession available: Ground 1 in Schedule 2 of the Housing Act 1988 (in Scotland, Ground 1 in Schedule 5 of the Housing (Scotland) Act 1988). To take advantage of this, you need to give the tenants notice that you may be recovering possession of the property under this ground (see chapter 9 for further information). But as most tenancy agreements nowadays are ASTs, there seems little point in using this ground, particularly as the accelerated possession procedure is no longer available for it.

Premiums

This is the term used where a sum of money is paid for a lease or tenancy. It is common practice with long leases. With short-term tenancies, they were specifically forbidden in the Rent Act 1977. They are not illegal now for ATs and ASTs under the Housing Act 1988.

In Scotland, it is unlawful to charge a premium or any form of fee or administration charge as a condition of granting a tenancy, as a consequence of the prohibition set out in s90 of the Rent (Scotland) Act 1984.

However, even where permitted, they are generally inadvisable, as if they are charged, the tenancy will have to be signed as a deed, they may affect the stamp duty payable, and they will affect the landlord's right to prohibit assignment (see chapter 6).

Succession rights

Having a tenancy is a property right, like owning a house or a flat on a long lease. If a tenant dies, his tenancy does not die with him. If a tenancy is a joint one (i.e. if more than one person has signed the tenancy agreement), then it will become the sole property of the remaining tenant. On the death of a sole tenant, provided the tenancy is one carrying succession rights, it will generally pass either to the spouse or, for Rent Act tenancies, provided certain conditions are met, to a member of the tenant's family (further information is given in chapter 10). It is beyond the scope of this book to go into the succession rules in any detail; if they are relevant to you, you should take legal advice.

Eviction of tenants and eviction notices

The eviction procedure and the various notices, Section 21 – notices requiring possession, and Section 8 – notices seeking possession, are discussed in chapter 9. In Scotland, the relevant notices are the Section 33 notice, the notice to quit and the AT6 notice.

The winds of change ...

This edition is being prepared in October 2015 after a number of legal changes have come into force for landlords.

- The Immigration Act 2014 brought in 'right to rent' immigration checks on tenants by landlords, which have been trialled in the West Midlands since December 2014. These will be rolled out to the rest of England (but not to Wales or Scotland, yet) from 1 February 2016.

- The Deregulation Act 2015 has brought in changes to the tenancy deposit rules which will be discussed in chapter 7.

- The Act has also brought in changes to Section 21 notices for tenancies which start or are renewed (other than as a statutory periodic tenancy) after 1 October 2015; see chapter 9 for details.

- New rules regarding smoke and carbon monoxide alarms have come into force from 1 October, which are discussed in chapter 3.

More changes are coming as a new Housing and Planning Bill and a new Immigration Bill have been published and are working their way through the legislative system.

Landlords should therefore ensure that they are kept informed, for example by joining a landlords' association or by subscribing to a suitable newsletter or journal, or via the author's online service at www.landlordlaw.co.uk and blog at www.landlordlawblog.co.uk.

In Scotland, the Antisocial Behaviour, Etc. (Scotland) Act 2004 includes provision for the registration of landlords with the local authority. This means that it is unlawful for you to let out residential property as a landlord unless the local authority approves of you. There are also penalties against the landlord if his property is occupied by antisocial tenants. The part of the Act affecting landlords is now in force. It affects all landlords and makes no distinction between short and long leases. It also affects resident landlords who have more than two lodgers. Existing and new landlords can contact their local authority to apply for registration, but they can be slow in responding. By far the best way to do register is online at www.landlordregistrationscotland.gov.uk.

The Housing (Scotland) Act 2006 introduces some major changes. It imposes new obligations on landlords to keep their properties maintained (see chapter 8). It also introduces a tenancy deposit scheme and new rules for HMOs.

The Private Rented Housing (Scotland) Act 2011 amends the landlord registration and HMO provisions and also provides for more information to be given to tenants at the start of the tenancy. There is a further Housing (Scotland) Bill which will extend the scope of registration further in order to cover letting agents as well. There will be a new registration scheme set up for letting agents and it will be an offence for a letting agent to operate without being registered. They will also not be permitted to charge fees for their work.

CHAPTER 2

Initial considerations

A lot of careful thought is required before letting a property or acquiring a property to let. Different considerations will apply, depending on the type of property you wish to let and the reasons for letting. For example:

- **Your own home.** There are two main reasons why people let their own homes: (1) they are going abroad for a period of time and will require it on their return; and (2) they are unable to sell their property, for example due to negative equity. If you intend to live in the property again yourself, you will want to be particularly careful with your choice of tenant, especially if your own furniture is left in the property.

- **Your second home.** You may have a second home which you wish to rent out as a holiday home to earn an income for the periods when you do not wish to stay in it yourself. As you will not, in the nature of things, have your main home local to the property, it is probably best to consider using one of the specialist holiday country cottage letting agencies, at least, to start with.

- **Inheritance.** You may have inherited a property, perhaps on the death of your parents, and be considering letting it for an income, rather than selling it. You have slightly more flexibility here because if the property is unsuitable for letting, you can sell it and buy another more viable property with the proceeds of the sale.

- **Buy-to-let.** You may be considering purchasing an investment property specifically for letting. See the section below for further details on this.

'Location, location, location'

When letting a property its location is all-important. On this will depend the type of tenant you are likely to attract and the level of rent you will be able to achieve. For example, take two identical properties:

1. One is in a popular residential area in a county town, positioned halfway between the university and the centre. This property will be very easy to let and should achieve an above average rent (provided it is in good condition).

2. The other is in a run-down part of a large 'inner-city' area, with high unemployment. This property will probably be very difficult to let unless you are prepared to take Housing Benefit tenants. Even then, particularly if the property is in an insalubrious part of town, you may find it impossible to let the property at all.

Even within a comparatively small area, conditions may change. A landlord of a property only a few miles from property 1, above, may find it harder to let or be unable to achieve such a good rent.

Also, conditions change over time. When letting student accommodation, for example, it is important that the property is available in the Spring when most students are looking to take on a tenancy for the following academic year. Also, rents may increase in the short term if a company in the area is looking to relocate a large number of staff who are all looking for rented accommodation.

The location of a property will also, to a large extent, determine the type of tenancy you will have. For example:

*   **'Good' areas.** These will be suitable for high-class assured shorthold tenancies (ASTs) (or short assured tenancies (SATs) in Scotland). These are usually the most trouble-free tenancies, as you can attract good quality tenants who will look after the property and pay promptly. Your initial investment, however, will be greater as the purchase price will probably be high and tenants will expect the property to be in good condition, with good quality fixtures and fittings.

*   **Country properties.** Often the most suitable type of letting here will be holiday lets. These can be remunerative, particularly if the property is attractive and in beautiful countryside with local holiday

attractions. Again, your investment may be high as holiday makers expect a high standard of comfort and facilities nowadays. Also, you may find that some items may need replacing frequently if holiday makers walk off with them.

• **Inner cities.** This is the type of area where you will find more HMOs and Housing Benefit tenants. These types of lettings are more time-consuming (particularly the HMOs) and you will probably have more problem tenants. However, with the right property and a careful choice of tenant, landlords can do well.

A landlord says ...

'If it is not good enough for you, it is probably not good enough for anyone else to live in.'

Other considerations

What is your intended type of tenant?

Different types of tenant will be attracted to different types of property. You should do some research into the market and decide what sector you will aim at, for example students, contract staff, Housing Benefit tenants. Some areas of the market are more profitable and some more labour-intensive. All will have different requirements which need to be borne in mind when purchasing a property and preparing it for letting.

Building or other work

The property as it stands may be unsuitable for letting, or for letting to the type of tenant you are seeking. For example, extensive alterations may be necessary if you intend the property to be an HMO, or you may want to improve the property's carbon footprint. You should cost very carefully the building work necessary, and any ongoing costs, making sure that you have considered all the legal requirements that landlords are subject to, for example his responsibilities to keep the property in repair (see chapter 3). Bear in mind also that a property let to tenants will generally need more redecoration and other work than your own home. If there is likely to be a rapid turnaround of tenants, you may well find that you are having to redecorate at least part of the property before every new, or every alternate new, letting if you wish to attract good quality tenants. If the cost is going to render the project economically unviable, it is better to find this out now rather than after the work has been done.

> **Note**
>
> If your property is an HMO, there are specific standards that you will have to comply with and you should contact your local authority. For further information, see chapter 4. You may also need planning permission.

Fixtures and fittings/furniture

Again, you need to consider the cost of fitting the property for letting, bearing in mind the product safety regulations discussed in chapter 3. Quality tenants will expect good quality fittings and 'white' goods (e.g. fridges, washing machines and cookers) in the property as standard, and will want furniture that is comfortable and attractive. Ensure that your budget is sufficient to provide for this.

Note that there are some companies which specialise in providing furniture suitable for buy-to-let properties – these firms can usually be found linked to landlord websites such as www.landlordzone.co.uk.

> **Tip**
>
> Ensure any 'white goods' you buy for the property have an 'A' energy rating.

> **A landlord says ...**
>
> 'I always ask myself, "Who is going to live in the property and if I were him, what would I want?"'

The availability of grants

Sometimes, local authority grants are available for improvement work on properties to be let. The availability of grants will vary from authority to authority and from time to time. You should speak to your local authority at the outset to see what is available. The type of grants that may be available include grants for property improvement/repairs, insulation, energy efficiency works, and for fire prevention works. Grants are normally awarded on an annual basis. If you are not successful one year, try again the next! Remember that if you do get a grant, you may have to pay at least part of it back if you sell the property within five years. Grants may also be available for landlords for energy efficiency improvements. Advice can be obtained from the Energy Saving Trust which operates advice centres across the UK. To contact your local centre call 0800 512 012.

A landlord says ...

'A ropey property in an area that the local authority wants smartening up will usually get a grant.'

Furnished or unfurnished?

For some types of letting you will have no choice; for example, students will not want unfurnished properties. Properties let unfurnished are more suitable for longer lets, for example to families who have their own furniture, and will generally achieve a lower rent. You will obtain a higher rent from furnished properties, especially if you are letting to professional people who require short-term accommodation because of work-related moves.

Achievable rent/financial considerations

Be realistic when considering rent. A property marketed at too high a rent is unlikely to find a tenant. When budgeting at this stage, it would be wise to allow for a slightly lower rent than you actually expect to achieve. Also, bear in mind that your actual earnings will be less than the monthly rent, even taking into account regular expenses such as mortgage payments. All rented properties will be empty for a period of time between tenants (known as 'voids'); also, you will have maintenance costs, agency fees (if you are letting via an agency) and probably other fees as well.

A landlord says ...

'I always budget on the basis that the property will only be let for ten months in the year.'

Tenant default

Always remember that even the best tenants can fall on hard times and can default on their rent. This may result in your having to evict them, which will mean legal expenses and a period without rent (as tenants rarely pay rent if they are being evicted). The likelihood of tenant default is far more likely in lower-quality HMOs, but it can occur in any type of property. Although tenant default is less likely in better quality lettings, when it does occur it will usually be more expensive – you are more likely to need a possession order and, of course, the rental you are losing is higher.

On the whole, most tenants are satisfactory. However, every landlord who lets for any period of time will have a bad tenant from time to time, and probably at least one tenant who will need evicting. Remember that 'Murphy's law' applies to residential letting as it does to every other area of life, and you will probably have your bad experience (if you have one) at the worst possible time. Try to guard against this and keep a special fund to pay for expenses should this type of thing happen. Note that solicitors' charges for standard repossession actions are in the region of £600–£1,000 plus VAT and the court issue fee (currently £280 or £250 if the courts online procedure is used). In Scotland the fee is £65–85 depending on the amount of rent arrears being claimed. When the Housing (Scotland) Bill comes into force the process for possession claims in Scotland will be different. They will be moved from the Sheriff's Court to the a new property tribunal. This specialist panel is expected to resolve these matters more quickly by using its expertise. Details of its operation and fees are not available at this stage.

Buy-to-let

Buy-to-let is popular and special buy-to-let mortgages are often available for investment properties. Many of these buy-to-let mortgage schemes are very good, and it is certainly worth considering using them to purchase a property for residential letting if you wish to invest but you do not have enough funds to buy outright. But the exercise should be carefully costed, particularly if the mortgage will be for a high percentage of the equity of the property.

When purchasing a property to let first you need to consider, 'What is my overall investment objective?' For example:

- You may be looking to purchase a house for your son while he is at university (a common arrangement is for the property to be let to the son and, say, three friends – the friends paying rent and the son living rent-free). This is a short-term objective, i.e. to provide accommodation for him for a limited period (normally three to four years) and then to sell the property, hopefully at a profit to reimburse you for the maintenance costs of supporting your son.

- Alternatively, you may be looking for an income to supplement a pension. This is a long-term objective.

What type of property should you purchase? Consider three things:

1. Your investment objective.

2. Whether you want rental income or capital growth as a priority. For example, if you have a good job, you may be looking for capital investment, whereas if you are retired, you may want to live on the income.

3. Can you visualise a situation where you will want to sell the property quickly? If the answer is yes, then you should look at properties in a prime location, as location sells. Do not look at good rental properties which will be difficult to sell.

You should note the following points:

- Do not buy in a poor location just to get in on the property market. What if you cannot let or sell it?

- Beware properties with structural faults. They may show a good rental return but may be impossible to sell. Leave these for the professional investor.

- Flats on long leases – these can be a good investment if you get the right one. However, there are many rogue landlords and poorly drafted leases, so be careful.

- Be very wary of very cheap properties, particularly in poor and run-down areas. You may be taking on a liability rather than an investment.

- Buy new properties rather than old, preferably with small gardens – they will generally need less maintenance.

- Go for smaller properties (not more than two to three bedrooms);

they will be easier to market and let than larger ones.

- Take proper advice, particularly if you are on a limited income.

Buying properties with existing tenants

If you are buying a property which is already tenanted, you should check very carefully the status of the existing tenancies. It may be wise to choose a solicitor who has some knowledge of residential lettings to do your conveyancing, rather than a cut-price firm where conveyancing is done on a 'conveyor belt' basis by unqualified staff. The following points are important:

- Establish the date when each tenancy **first** started.

- Make sure you obtain a copy of the initial tenancy agreement as well as the most recent one (if there has been more than one).

- If the tenancy began between 15 January 1989 and 28 February 1997, make sure that a Section 20 notice (explained in chapter 1) was served on the tenant and that you have a copy of the notice that was served and evidence that it was served prior to the tenancy being entered into (as otherwise you will not be able to evict the tenant under the shorthold ground). Ideally, you should have a statutory declaration from the person who served the notice on the tenant which exhibits a copy of the notice served. In Scotland, check to see if it is a short assured tenancy or an assured tenancy, and make sure that an AT5 notice has been served.

- If the tenant first went into the property before 15 January 1989, then he will be a Rent Act tenant and you will find it very difficult, if not impossible, to evict him, should this become necessary. Also, you will not be able to charge more than the registered 'fair rent', which may be lower than the current market rent.

- Beware if there is no documentation regarding the tenancy, and be particularly wary of properties bought at auction or as a result of mortgage repossessions, which often have no documentation and tenancies with unclear status.

- Investigate any tenancy deposit carefully. Ensure that you are going to be provided with the money taken as the deposit or the sum is being taken off the purchase price, and confirm that the deposit was registered in accordance with the relevant requirements at the time it was taken.

Tip

If you are considering buying a property at auction, *Buying Bargains at Property Auctions* published by Lawpack, will be very helpful.

Local authority assistance

Because of the pressure on local authorities to rehouse the homeless and the reduction of their housing stock due to the right to buy, local authorities are becoming more reliant on the private sector to fulfil their statutory obligations. They are, therefore, often keen to assist landlords to bring more properties into use. Many local authorities have a special section looking at bringing empty homes back into use and there are sometimes grants available to bring the property up to the required standard. For example, flats above shops are often targeted, although if they have not been used for residential purposes before, they may require planning permission for the change of use. Often local authorities will agree to enter into a leasing agreement with a landlord, whereby the landlord is paid rent by the local authority who will then be able to use the property to house homeless families. This is often attractive to landlords, as the rent is guaranteed by the local authority and it will also maintain the property.

Even if the local authority is not able to enter into a leasing agreement, it will be able to assist in finding tenants and will often have a damage deposit guarantee scheme, to help prospective tenants who cannot afford to pay. New landlords, and experienced landlords seeking to purchase property in a new area, are therefore advised to contact their local authority to see what is available.

Many local authorities are keen to work with local landlords and will have a landlords' forum which landlords may find useful to join. Local authorities may also run an accreditation scheme that landlords can also join (see more on this in chapter 3).

Landlords' associations

Check to see if there is a landlords' association in your area. It may be prepared to give you some initial advice. If you decide to take the plunge and become a landlord, your landlords' association will be invaluable. You will normally, however, have to agree to comply with the association's code of practice as a condition of membership. Benefits of membership generally include:

- Regular meetings where you can hear speakers on subjects of interest to landlords and have an opportunity to speak to other, perhaps more experienced, landlords.

- Information on the latest housing legislation, rules and good practice.

- Practical advice and information.

- A list of approved suppliers, many of whom will offer discounts to members.

- Competitive property and contents insurance cover for members.

- A regular newsletter.

- The respect which usually flows from being a member of a recognised professional body.

Some associations are involved in running accreditation schemes, perhaps in conjunction with the local authority, college or university. The larger landlords' associations will also lobby government on issues relevant to private landlords, so by becoming a member of these you may be able to help influence government decisions affecting the private landlord.

Tip

The largest landlords' associations are the National Landlords Association, the Residential Landlords Association and the Eastern Landlords Association. Other smaller local associations are listed online.

Landlord forums

Landlords can now often get support and help from other landlords via online forums. One of the best known is Property Tribes at www.propertytribes.com. There are also forums on the LandlordZONE website, www.landlordzone.co.uk and on Property118, www.property118.com.

You will also find various landlord groups on Facebook and LinkedIn. Although these can be helpful, be aware that some of the people posting will not be experienced landlords and you may need to take some of the posts with a pinch of salt.

CHAPTER 3

Preparation of the property

Before preparing your property for letting, you should first ensure that you are legally entitled to let it to tenants.

Permission for letting

This may be necessary, for example:

- If the property is leasehold, you will need to check your lease carefully. Usually in a long lease you will need your own landlord's permission before subletting, or you may have to give notice. You should ensure that any terms in your lease are complied with. Long lease landlords will usually seek to charge a fee as a part of giving consent. They can do this as long as it is reasonable; for a standard assured shorthold tenancy, the sum should be less than £200.

- If there is a mortgage on the property, you will need to obtain the lender's permission to let. This is normally granted, although some lenders will only give consent subject to a small increase in the interest rate on the loan. If you do not obtain the lender's consent, strictly speaking you will be in breach of the mortgage agreement and they may be entitled to call in the loan. Any conditions imposed by the lender should be complied with.

Planning permission

This is not normally necessary unless you are 'developing' a property (e.g. converting a single home to a house in multiple occupation (HMO). You should not require planning permission to let to a single family, however large, but any letting to sharers may require planning permission depending on the policy of the local planning authority. The situation is slightly different in different parts of the country and therefore the best thing you can do is to speak to the planning officer at your local authority.

If planning permission is needed, the Planning Officer will probably be looking at the availability of parking, so do ensure that there is adequate parking at the property. He will also be considering such things as fire prevention, sound proofing and compliance with the HMO regulations. If you are developing an HMO, even if it is not one that requires licensing, it is important that you comply with all the requirements, as the environmental health department will inevitably find out about the property sooner or later (e.g. from the Benefit Office when your tenants claim benefit). If you do not have planning permission, they will then be serving enforcement notices on you. When planning permission is granted, it is important that you do not exceed the permitted number of tenants.

In Scotland (although not in England) it is a ground to refuse the granting of an HMO licence that the correct planning permission has not been obtained. Therefore, it is important to ensure that you have met the requirements of the planning department.

Remember that if you are carrying out any building works, you will also need to comply with building regulations. You should not confuse building regulations with planning permission; the two are separate and both must be complied with.

Tip

Watch out for agricultural restrictions on properties on farms; their use may be limited to occupation by farm workers.

Renovations and repairs

Once you have dealt with any preliminary legal requirements, you then need to put the property into a proper condition, before it is let; for example:

- Cutting costs and not having the property in a good state of repair will not attract good tenants, which may result in problems later in the tenancy. Most people are not prepared to put up with poor quality accommodation nowadays.

- You may not have access during the letting.

- If the property is in poor repair, you will be vulnerable to claims by the tenants (who may be eligible for Legal Aid), who can apply for an injunction (or interdict in Scotland) and/or damages, or you may have an improvement notice served on you by the local authority.

- It is easier to ensure that the property is left in a good condition after the tenants leave if it is in a good condition when they arrive. Also, as you will find out later when we look at the 'anti-retaliatory eviction' measures in the Dereglation Act 2015 (England only), if the property is in poor condition you may find that you are unable to serve a Section 21 notice on your tenants.

- You will have complied with your legal obligations, which will make it difficult for tenants to justify any non-compliance with their obligations (such as payment of rent).

A landlord has a duty to put a property into proper repair before it is let to tenants and to keep it in proper repair once it is let. Under the Landlord and Tenant Act 1985 and Housing (Scotland) Act 2006, private residential landlords are responsible for:

- the structure and exterior of the dwelling;

- installations for the supply of water, gas, electricity and sanitation;

- basins, sinks, baths and other sanitary installations;

- heating and hot water installations.

If a tenancy forms part of a larger building which the landlord owns or has control over, then he is also responsible for keeping in repair the structure and exterior, and for keeping in repair and proper working order any installations located in any part of the building and which directly or indirectly serve the installations in the tenanted property. For example, in a block of flats the landlord will have to keep the common parts in repair, and also the other flats, but only if any disrepair interferes with his tenants' use of their flat and the common parts they are entitled to use.

Note also that there are specific additional standards which HMO properties will need to meet. You should speak to your local authority about this as different authorities have different requirements. For the basic standards, see chapter 4.

For major works, you may wish to consider employing a qualified architect or surveyor to oversee it. As discussed above, you may be eligible for a local authority grant for works, particularly if you are converting a property to an HMO. You will usually need two written estimates of the cost. As always with building works, you need to be careful with your choice of builder. You may wish to consider using one who belongs to a trade association which operates a guarantee scheme, such as those run by the Building Employees Confederation or the Federation of Master Builders.

A landlord says ...

'You need to get a property right from the outset – it is very difficult to get routine improvements done if tenants are in occupation.'

Local authority powers

It is not often realised that local authorities have a duty to ensure that residential property in their area is in good condition and can use draconian powers to force property owners to bring their properties up to standard.

In England, these powers and duties have now been amended by the Housing Act 2004, which brought in a new method of assessing properties. The old fitness standards have now been replaced by an evidence based Housing Health and Safety Rating System (HHSRS). Under this system, local authority Environmental Health Officers (EHOs) will, when doing an inspection, assess properties under 29 categories of housing hazard. The EHO will give each hazard a rating, which will be expressed through a numerical score which falls within a band. There are ten bands. Scores in Bands A to C are Category 1 hazards and scores in Bands D to J are Category 2 hazards. These scores will be entered into a computer program which will work out the result of the property inspection. If the property has Category 1 hazards, the authority will be under a duty to take action. If there are only Category 2 hazards, then the local authority will use its discretion to decide whether to take action or not.

The HHSRS assessment is based on the risk to the potential occupant who is most vulnerable to that hazard (referred to in the Regulations as the 'relevant occupier'). However, the actual occupier of the property may not be in this vulnerable group. For example, stairs constitute a greater risk to the elderly, so for assessing hazards relating to stairs they (i.e. the elderly) are considered the most vulnerable, even though the property may actually be occupied by students. The reasoning behind this is that a dwelling that is safe for those most vulnerable to a hazard is safe for all. If it is assessed on the basis of the current occupier, the property would have to be reassessed for every new occupier, for example if a group of students is replaced by a family with young children.

It will largely be left to the discretion of local authorities as to whether they take action (assuming that there are no Category 1 hazards) and if so, the action that they will take. So, using the example above, if the stairs are considered a Category 2 hazard but the property is occupied by students, the local authority may not consider it appropriate to take action at that stage. However, their decision will be affected by statutory guidance which will be issued by the relevant government department from time to time.

The most normal enforcement procedure will be the issuing of an improvement notice, which will require the property owner to carry out works to deal with the hazard identified. Needless to say, any landlords who are issued with an improvement notice should ensure that the works are done as soon as possible. However, if, for any reason, they consider that the notice should not have been issued, there is an appeal process.

It is likely that the HHSRS will impact mostly on landlords of HMO properties which need to be licensed, as all licensed properties will be inspected at least once during the licence period. However, the standards apply to all properties and not just HMOs.

Further information on the HHSRS and guidance for landlords can be obtained from www.communities.gov.uk.

Note

The Deregulation Act 2015 renders Section 21 notices unenforceable if the property is in disrepair and this is confirmed by the local authority serving an improvement notice. This came into force (in England only) on 1 October 2015, for tenancies which began or were renewed after that date.

In Scotland, the Housing (Scotland) Act 2006 amends the law regarding the landlord's duties to repair and maintain let property.

The landlord is required to meet the repairing standard at the start of the tenancy and at all times during the tenancy. The repairing standard, as defined in the Act, is as follows:

1. The property must be wind and watertight and fit for human habitation.

2. The structure and exterior of the property, including the drains, gutters and external pipes, should be in a reasonable state of repair and in proper working order.

3. The installations in the property, including gas, electricity, sanitation, space, heating and water heating, should be in a reasonable state of repair and in proper working order.

4. The fixtures and fittings and appliances in the property should be in a reasonable state of repair and in proper working order.

5. The furnishings should be able to be used safely for the purpose for which they were designed.

6. There should be satisfactory provision made for the detecting of fire and for giving warnings, i.e. smoke detectors should be fitted.

The landlord will be required before the start of the tenancy to provide to the tenant written information about the landlord's duties to comply with the repairing standard. A template letter which includes this information can be found at www.prhpscotland.gov.uk.

If the landlord fails to comply with the repairing standard, the tenant can apply to the Private Rented Housing Panel (PHRP). If it agrees that the landlord is failing to meet his obligations, it has the power to issue an enforcement order giving a reasonable period, which must not be less than 21 days, within which to carry out work which will be specified in the order. Failure to comply with the order can lead to the panel granting a rent relief order which can be for up to 90 per cent of the rent and failure to comply with the order is also made a criminal offence punishable by a fine. Once the Housing (Scotland) Bill comes into force, the local authority will also be able to apply to the PRHP if a landlord is in breach of the repairing standard, reducing the problem of tenants being afraid or uninterested in making applications.

Building regulations

Before carrying out any building work, you need to check whether building regulations apply. If they do, you will have to obtain approval of your proposed works before they start and they will have to be inspected after completion. Your architect/surveyor/builder should be able to arrange this for you.

Heating

It will be difficult to let the property unless it has proper heating, and this generally means central heating. Providing proper heating will also mean that tenants are less likely to use their own heating devices, such as gas cylinder heaters, which may be dangerous. It is often a good idea to specify in the tenancy agreement that the heating facilities provided (e.g. central heating) must be used and to prohibit other forms of heating, particularly oil and gas cylinder heaters which can be dangerous if not properly used.

Many old methods of heating will be inefficient and will result in a high carbon footprint for the property. If you want to install a new heating system, you should obtain advice on the most energy efficient system. Free advice can be obtained from the Energy Saving Trust on 0800 512 012.

Note

One of the hazards referred to above in the HSSRS is 'excess cold', which can be surprisingly dangerous, especially for the elderly. Landlords should be careful, therefore, to ensure that proper heating facilities are provided.

Condensation and damp

This is mentioned here as it is probably the most common complaint about properties nationwide. It can often be avoided by landlords installing proper heating, insulation and ventilation. However, condensation is sometimes caused by tenants not heating the property and not opening the windows. If this is likely to be a problem, it might be a good idea for the tenancy agreement to provide that the property should be heated to a certain specified level in the winter.

In many cases, excessive condensation and damp is caused by the design of the property. This is not something the tenant can complain about under the statutory repairing covenants and landlords cannot be forced to do extra works on that basis. However, they need to be aware that if the damp or condensation is severe, a tenant can bring a prosecution under the Environmental Protection Act 1990, if he is able to claim that the condition of the property constitutes a 'statutory nuisance'. The process involves serving a formal notice on the landlord and then waiting 21 days before commencing court action. Landlords served with council or tenant notices about damp and mould should act quickly on specialist advice.

Note

One of the hazards covered in the HHSRS is damp and mould growth.

Gas regulations

The Gas Safety (Installation and Use) Regulations 1998

These are to ensure the safety of all gas appliances in all let properties and must be strictly adhered to. Badly maintained gas appliances can kill. From April 2009, the company which gas installers need to be registered with changed from CORGI to the Gas Safe Register, and the Gas Safe Register is now the official body for gas safety in Great Britain and the Isle of Man. You can find out more about them, and also find a Gas Safe-registered installer, from their website at www.gassaferegister.co.uk.

- All gas appliances (including mobile gas heaters) must be properly installed by a Gas Safe-registered plumber (see the Appendix for details). Where a new installation has been carried out by a registered person, then the installation certificate will be acceptable as a safety certificate for 12 months.

- Before a property is let, and annually thereafter, all gas appliances and installations must be checked by a Gas Safe-registered plumber. The obligation is to renew the gas safety certificate every 12 months and this must be done before the current certificate expires.

- A copy of the gas certificate stating that a check has been done and detailing any work done must be handed to a tenant at the start of a tenancy and provided to him annually thereafter (within 28 days of the annual check being completed).

- For properties, such as holiday lets, where occupancy is under 28 days, a copy of the safety check record should be posted in a prominent position in the premises.

- A landlord cannot delegate maintenance or safety checks to a tenant.

- All gas certificates must be kept for at least two years, but landlords are advised to keep them for at least six years, just in case they are needed as evidence in any claim brought in respect of the property. It is acceptable to scan the certificates into a computer or other electronic storage medium, provided they can be printed back out onto paper.

Remember, the landlord is ultimately responsible for the safety of all gas appliances in properties let by him; if a tenant dies of carbon monoxide poisoning, the landlord will be prosecuted for manslaughter. The only way you can avoid this happening is by ensuring that comprehensive checks are carried out each year by a Gas Safe-registered plumber authorised to do the work, and to ensure that all complaints from the tenant are dealt with immediately. Keep proper records of everything so you can prove, if necessary, that you have complied with the law.

The regulations are administered and enforced by the Health & Safety Executive. The obligations of landlords are summarised in a leaflet called A Guide to Landlords' Duties, available free from HSE Books. Breach of the regulations is a criminal offence punishable either by a fine of up to £5,000 for each offence, or an unlimited fine/imprisonment if the case is referred to the Crown Court.

If a tenant will not permit access for the carrying out of a gas safety check the HSE prosecution guidance currently states that they will not prosecute provided at least three attempts have been made to obtain access, and evidence is kept of this.

Note

In England only, where a tenancy is created or renewed on or after 1 October 2015, landlords will be unable to serve a valid Section 21 notice if the gas safety certificate has not been served on the tenants at the start of the tenancy (although the regulations do provide for late service provided this is before the service of the section 21 notice).

Problems to watch out for:

- Dust and detritus in a gas appliance which can cause it to become unsafe. A sign of this is when the colour of the flame changes to a smoky yellow.

- Black soot deposits around gas appliances.

- Cracks in the cement blocks found in older fires and mobile heaters.

- Poor ventilation, caused by either a blocked flue or ventilation in a room (e.g. air bricks) becoming blocked, which can cause a build-up of carbon monoxide in the air.

- Gas leaks (e.g. if gas pipes become damaged). It is important to ensure that vulnerable pipes are protected.

Tip

For further advice, ring the HSE Gas Safety Advice Line on 0800 300 363.

Electricity

At the time of writing, there are no specific regulations requiring certification for electrical wiring/installations in rented property (except where the property is an HMO). However, the landlord has a general duty to provide a safe environment and is strongly advised to have the electrical installations regularly checked. Remember that a common cause of fire is faulty electrical installations and the landlord can be found liable to the tenant for any losses. You will generally be protected from claims by tenants if you have the property inspected before the tenants go in, and deal with all complaints promptly.

If you intend to let to students, a students' union or accommodation office will generally require all properties on their list to have an annual inspection report covering the electrical installation at the property from an electrical contractor who is a member of the National Inspection Council for Electrical Installation Contracting (NICEIC). Further information can be obtained from your local college students' union or accommodation office.

Note

Electrical installations in HMO properties must be inspected and tested at least every five years by a qualified electrician and a certificate must be obtained.

A landlord says ...

'I was glad I had arranged for an electrical inspection when the Inspector found a live wire in one of the walls, due to unauthorised wall lights having been installed and then removed by the previous tenants. This could have got me into serious trouble if one of my tenants had been electrocuted!'

Fire safety

This is particularly important for the larger HMOs, where there are strict regulations – for further information, speak to your local authority. However, it is important that this is considered for all properties, if only to protect your investment.

Consider the following points when preparing a property for letting:

- All landlords are required by law to ensure that there is an adequate means of escape in case of fire.

- Try to protect the staircase, so that everyone can get out in an emergency, by fitting self-closing doors to all rooms.

- Fit smoke detectors to warn in the event of a fire. For HMOs, these need to be interlinked, mains-powered smoke detectors. For large HMOs, the smoke alarms need to be linked to a commercial fire alarm system. (See below for the rules on smoke alarms for properties in England.)

- It should be possible for the front door to be opened at all times from the inside. Cylinder locks are better than mortice locks, which need to be unlocked with a key. If you feel a mortice lock is essential, get one with a thumb turn from the inside. Also possible but less satisfactory (because it can get lost or be stolen) is to have a spare key hanging by the door.

- Give new tenants an information pack regarding fire safety.

- Place notices in HMOs showing exit routes in the case of fire, and the location of the nearest phone for calling the fire brigade.

- Consider a fire blanket and small dry powder extinguisher for the kitchen (if the property is an HMO, discuss this with the Fire Officer).

- Try to make escape routes (e.g. corridors) 'fire sterile': do not have anything that can burn on the walls – use emulsion paint rather than wallpaper or hessian covering.

For larger HMOs, you should also consider:

- Emergency lighting (this may be mandatory for some local authorities).

- Arranging means of escape through adjacent buildings.

- Fire-retardant curtains.

Take proper advice on fire safety and get the necessary work done before the tenants move in. Speak first to your local Environmental Health Officer; however; your local fire brigade will often be pleased to advise, too. Lawpack's *Landlord's Fire Risk Assessment Kit is* available from www.lawpack.co.uk.

Smoke and carbon monoxide (CO) alarms

From 1 October 2015, **all** rental properties in England must have smoke alarms fitted on all storeys with living accommodation and CO alarms in rooms with a solid fuel-burning appliance (e.g. wood burning stove). These must be tested on the first day of the tenancy – after that, it is up to the tenants to maintain them. A guide can be found on the gov.uk website at https://goo.gl/EPZiDS.

Water

If a property is converted into flats, the water company may have the right to install water meters. Problems may arise with apportionment and payment of water bills if, for example, two or more flats have a shared water heater. Ideally, each flat should have its own water meter. Often, for example in HMOs, the landlord pays the water bills; if the water is metered, this may mean large bills for you, as tenants rarely economise on something that is free to them. If they are annoyed with you for any reason, they may even leave taps running deliberately. A tenant paying the bills themselves with a tenancy of six months or more is entitled to have a water meter fitted into the property, irrespective of the landlord's wishes.

An HMO landlord says ...

'If utility bills are in the name of tenants, they will often do a runner when the bills come in. I am not responsible for the bills, but I have all the bother of having to find another tenant.'

There have been suggestions that landlords should be held responsible if their tenants leave without paying the water bills but as yet this is not the case. However, landlords should co-operate with the water authorities if they are chasing an unpaid bill. In England, legislation has been passed (but is not yet in force) which requires landlords to obtain a forwarding address for a tenant after the tenancy has ended, and provides that where they fail to take reasonable steps to do so then the water company can ask the landlord to pay any outstanding water bill.

It will not normally be considered a breach of the Data Protection Act if you assist utilities by providing forwarding addresses for your tenants, although it may be an idea to state this somewhere in your terms and conditions, either in your tenancy agreement (although most printed tenancy forms do not include this) or perhaps in a separate letter or notice. In Wales, there is now legislation requiring landlords to provide the full names and dates of birth of all occupiers, along with the date that they first occupied the premises. A portal for landlords to do this is at www.landlordtap.com.

Energy efficiency

Landlords must obtain an Energy Performance Certificate from an accredited energy assessor and provide a copy to the tenant at the start of the tenancy. Under rules in England only for tenancies created or renewed on or after 1 October 2015, a valid Section 21 notice cannot be served unless this has been done – in the same way as discussed above for gas safety certificates.

The energy efficiency and environmental impact of the property will be rated on a scale from A to G (A is the most efficient and G the least). Current running costs for heating, hot water and lighting will also be shown on the certificate, together with recommended energy saving improvements.

People are very aware of their responsibilities to the environment nowadays, and a property with a low carbon footprint (and thus low heating and other expenses) will probably be more popular with tenants. Landlords are therefore advised to get any remedial work done before the certificate is obtained.

Grants may be available for landlords for energy efficiency improvements and there are also tax incentives. Advice on this and other matters can be obtained from the Energy Saving Trust; to contact your local centre call 0800 512 012 or see their website at www.energysavingtrust.org.uk.

Note

From April 2018, it will be unlawful to let residential properties with an F or G EPC rating. Landlords with low energy efficiency rated properties are advised to make energy efficiency improvements if they want to continue letting beyond April 2018.

The Green Deal

This is a government scheme which will allow landlords (and also owner occupiers) to have energy efficiency improvements done to their property, with the cost of this being recouped from the utility bills. Landlords interested in this will find full details on the government website www.gov.uk/green-deal-energy-saving-measures. There are also articles about its effect on landlords on the landlord association websites.

Fitting out the property

To a certain extent, the standard of fittings and furnishings will depend upon the type of tenant you are catering for. However, generally standards have increased in recent years and you may find it difficult to find good tenants if the property does not have good quality fittings and furniture. Obviously they should all comply with the product safety regulations described below.

Most people will now require as standard good quality 'white goods' (e.g. cookers, fridges, washing machines, etc.). White goods should have an energy efficiency rating of A and preferably be an energy saving recommended product carrying the 'Energy saving recommended' logo. You can find out more about this scheme and recommended retailers from the Energy Saving Trust website at www.energysavingtrust.org.uk (search for appliances).

Furniture should be attractive but hard wearing. Even if you are letting a property unfurnished, it will need to be carpeted and have curtains.

Note that there are companies which specialise in fittings and furniture for buy-to-let properties. You can generally find these on the internet; for example, via landlords' websites such as www.landlordzone.co.uk.

A landlord says ...

'It is best to use good quality carpeting as cheap carpets stain easily and are often difficult to clean.'

Product safety regulations

These regulations generally apply when a landlord is letting a property as a commercial venture. This includes properties which are being let via an agent. As a matter of good practice, however, the regulations should be complied with in all cases. If a landlord is letting his own home, say while he is working abroad for a year leaving his own furniture in the property, then the regulations will probably not apply.

The various product safety regulations apply to anything supplied as part of a property, but not permanently fixed.

A Trading Standards Officer says ...

'If in doubt, chuck it out.'

Furniture and furnishings

The Furniture and Furnishings (Fire) (Safety) Regulations apply to all furniture and soft furnishings, which must be fire-safety compliant. Items covered include padded headboards, sofas, mattresses, pillows, cushions, nursery furniture, and cloth covers on seats. Make sure that all items carry the proper label.

Items which are exempt are furniture made before 1950 (and reupholstery of furniture made before that date), curtains, carpets, duvets and sheets.

There is a very helpful guide to the regulations published by the Department of Business, Enterprise and Regulatory Reform, which can be obtained from your local Trading Standards Office, which will also be able to give you general advice.

Electrical equipment

The Electrical Equipment (Safety) Regulations control the supply of electrical equipment. This covers all electrical goods, i.e. kettles, TVs, fires, fridges, etc., which must be safe. It is best to have them tested by a bona fide qualified electrician, preferably annually. Keep records of all inspections and testing, with lists of the items inspected and details of their condition. Things to watch out for include:

- Plugs, which need to be sleeved.

- Old cookers, as the plates may become live if the insulation is old.

- Bare or damaged wire on leads.

- Small moveable objects which are more likely to be damaged through wear and tear.

Electrical items also need to comply with the Plugs and Sockets Safety Regulations; if they were purchased new recently, this should not be a problem.

Tip

These regulations do not apply to the tenant's own furniture and possessions. However, these must be removed when they leave the property.

The General Product Safety Regulations

The General Product Safety Regulations control the supply of general consumer products. These regulations cover general problems in properties, such as missing rungs in ladders, stepladders with faulty locking devices, and slippery carpets. Anything supplied in the property needs to be safe.

You need to ensure this, not only because you might become liable for prosecution under the regulations, but also because you might otherwise become liable for a civil claim for damages, if someone is injured as a result of the unsafe item. You should therefore always ensure that there are no unsafe items when properties are let, and make sure that repairs are done quickly, once they are brought to your attention by your tenant.

Disabled tenants

If you let to disabled tenants, note that they have a right to ask you to make reasonable adjustments for them, e.g. by providing small ramps for wheelchair users. However, they are not normally entitled to demand expensive adaptations. In particular, landlords and managers of rented premises cannot be forced to take any steps which involve the removal or alteration of physical features of the property. However, the regulations have set out things which are not to count as 'physical features' and which a disabled tenant is entitled to ask to have done. These are:

- the replacement or provision of any signs or notices;

- the replacement of any taps or door handles;

- the replacement, provision or adaptation of any door bell or door entry system;

- changes to the colour of any surface (such as, a wall or door).

In addition, landlords cannot unreasonably withhold consent from disabled tenants who need to make physical adjustments to their homes for disability-related reasons. However, the tenant must pay for the alterations and must ask permission from the landlord. This right of individual tenants to make adjustments will not apply to the 'common parts' of properties such as stairs or hallways of communal blocks of flats.

For more information see the relevant section of the Equality and Human Rights Commission website at www.equalityhumanrights.com. Note that there may be changes in this area of law, so landlords should be on the look out for information.

Smoking

It is a matter for you whether you allow your tenants to smoke in the property. If you do permit smoking, you should arrange for smoke detectors to be installed (although ideally these should be installed anyway). However, note that common areas (e.g. hallways and shared parts of HMOs) must now be smoke free under the regulations. You should inform tenants of this and arrange for the appropriate notices to be displayed.

... and finally

The best way to deal with all these regulations is to draw up a full inventory of all upholstered furniture, electrical equipment and general consumer products in the property, and make a note of their general condition. You should then make sure that all of any identified problems are dealt with before the property is let. This should also be done every time the property is vacated before reletting. Keep records of all checks (e.g. electrical checks) done, repairs and items replaced. Keep all invoices and receipts (you should also keep these to claim against tax).

The Trading Standards Office is the prosecuting authority for offences under these regulations. However, it will normally want to work with a landlord to put things right and will only prosecute as a last resort. It is always happy to advise and new landlords should contact their local office at an early stage as it usually has useful advice/fact sheets which landlords will find helpful.

'In our experience, the better the condition of the property at the start of the tenancy, the less likelihood there is that the property will be left in a poor condition at the end of the tenancy.'

Insurance

You need to be sure that your insurance is suitable for rented property. If you are letting your own home, do not rely on your ordinary household insurance. In particular, ensure that your insurer knows that the property is rented. With insurance, you have a duty of good faith to tell the insurer all relevant factors. If you do not, the insurer can refuse to pay when a claim is made.

Even if you are only letting rooms in your own home, you need to check that you are adequately insured.

Insurance for rented properties generally needs to cover the following:

- The structure of the property.
- Landlord's contents, fittings and fixtures (the tenant generally insures his own possessions).
- Public liability – this is to cover you in the event of tenants or members of the general public making a claim in respect of personal injury or death, or damage to their possessions. Insurers recommend that this should be for a minimum of five million pounds. This sounds a lot, but claims from several people, particularly if they are seriously injured, could be extremely expensive.
- Loss of rent following damage to the property.

You might also wish to consider insurance cover for:

- The cost of finding alternative accommodation for your tenants.
- Legal expenses.
- Non-payment of rent (a rent guarantee policy).

If you take out any of these policies, it is wise to read the small print, which will usually specify actions that need to be taken before a claim can be made. For example, letters demanding payment of unpaid rent will normally need to be sent to the tenant within a specified period of time. If this is not done, cover may be refused.

If you are considering letting to asylum seekers, Housing Benefit tenants or students, be sure to check that the policy does not exclude these. Remember that tenants' circumstances can change; for example, they may go on benefit without you knowing about it. However, this would not stop your insurers refusing to pay when a claim is made.

As with all insurance, you also need to insure for the correct sum. If the structure of the property is underinsured, this will affect payouts not only when there is total destruction of the property but also for smaller claims, as insurers will say that you have only insured a proportion of the property. Your surveyor will be able to advise you of the current rebuilding costs.

Most landlords' associations will have a special insurance policy available for members and this is usually excellent value. If this is not available, you should consult an independent insurance broker for advice before taking out insurance.

There are now several insurance companies offering specialist policies for private residential landlords.

Note that if your tenancy agreement seeks to make the tenant liable should he breach the terms of your insurance policy (e.g. if he causes the premiums to increase) then you will need to provide a copy of the insurance policy, or an extract of the relevant parts, to the tenant. If you do not, the clause in the tenancy agreement may be invalid.

So far as tenants' property is concerned, they are responsible for arranging for their own insurance and it is not normal for their possessions to be covered by the landlord's policy. They should be informed of this and advised to take out their own protection. However, do note that landlords cannot **require** tenants to take out insurance; this is a matter for them.

Note

If either you or your tenant have an unspent criminal conviction, this can in some cases void your insurance. Make sure you check with your insurance company about this.

It may be wise to ask your tenants to complete an application form which includes a question asking them to confirm whether or not they have any convictions. This should be sufficient to discharge your duty to your insurers on this point.

Rent

If you are a new landlord, it may be best to take professional advice when setting rent levels for the first time. Multiple occupancy (e.g. renting individual rooms in a property, to students say, on separate agreements) will often achieve a higher rent than letting the property as a whole; certainly if you are letting to tenants on Housing Benefit this will normally be the case. But if the landlord lets to a group of tenants on an agreement, he has the protection of joint and several liability (see chapter 1). Sources of information for local rental levels include properties let by other agents, local papers and the internet (e.g. letting agents and landlords' association websites).

The rental market is different from the selling market. Rental levels can fluctuate from one month to the next and from one area to another.

Tip

Be particularly wary when taking advice on local rent figures from sales agents, especially in new-build property. These figures are often inflated and bear more resemblance to the expected mortgage payments for the property price, than to the local rent figure!

If you are including Council Tax and any utilities in the rent (as will often be the case with HMOs), you should, particularly if the property is being let to tenants on Housing Benefit, apportion the rent between pure rental and payment for each individual service or tax. Your tenancy agreement should make provision for the rent to increase in line with services or Council Tax.

Accreditation

Some local authorities, landlords' associations and student bodies are running accreditation schemes for landlords. Landlords who are members have to ensure that their properties meet the prescribed standards and comply with any other requirements of the scheme. They can then advertise their properties as accredited and take advantage of any local promotion of the scheme, for example through universities for student accommodation. Another advantage of membership is that training is also sometimes available for landlords as part of the scheme. Many schemes, particularly those run by local authorities, will include a landlords' forum where landlords can make their views known to the local authority and 'network' with other landlords. Plus many local authority licence fees will be lower for accredited landlords.

Further information and details of accreditation schemes near you can be obtained from the Accreditation Network, which has a website at www.anuk.org.uk, or contact your local authority. Note that the largest accreditation scheme is the London Landlords' Accreditation Scheme, which covers all London boroughs and which provides training. For more information see the website at www.londonlandlords.org.uk.

Note

From 23 November 2015, the Housing (Wales) Act 2014 will introduce new obligations on landlords and letting agents in Wales. Landlords and agents will have one year from that date to register and apply for a licence. If you are based in Wales, you can read about this on the Rent Smart Wales website at www.rentsmart.gov.wales/en.

CHAPTER 4

Houses in multiple occupation

For many years, some types of property, where a number of people who are unrelated share accommodation, have been classed as houses in multiple occupation, generally known as 'HMOs'. Traditionally these types of property are more likely to be problematic, particularly the large HMOs, mainly because there are often large numbers of people who do not know each other living in close proximity. Also, HMO tenants tend to be transitory and there is often a high turnover.

HMOs (particularly the larger HMOs) need a lot of management and are probably best managed by the landlord rather than a letting agent. Landlords should visit these properties regularly, in many cases it will be advisable to visit on a weekly basis; for example, where rooms in the property are let to different tenants under separate tenancy agreements. One bad tenant can affect the whole household, and the landlord has a duty of care to his other tenants. An HMO landlord needs to know what is going on in his property.

For some time there have been additional regulations which relate to the running of HMOs, and local authorities have had greater powers to become involved in regulating these properties. Since the Housing Act 2004 has come into force, the law relating to HMOs has changed substantially, in particular:

- a change in the definition of an HMO means that more properties than before will now come into the HMO category;

- a mandatory licensing scheme has now come into effect whereby larger HMOs are now required to obtain a licence from their local authority;

- local authorities now have the power to set up additional licensing schemes for other types of HMO property;

- new regulations have been passed relating to the management of HMOs replacing the earlier 1990 regulations.

This chapter considers the special rules that relate to HMO properties.

Note

Some HMOs will need planning permission. This is discussed in chapter 3. If you are not sure whether or not your property will need planning permission, speak to your local authority planning officer.

What is an HMO?

The legal definition of an HMO is now set out in Section 254 onwards in the Housing Act 2004 (in Scotland, Section 125 of the Housing (Scotland) Act 2006). You can read the Acts in full on the internet in the legislation section and on the UK Statute Law Database at www.statutelaw.gov.uk. It is a very long definition and it is not practical to reproduce it here.

Basically, if you have one of the following, it will be an HMO:

- An entire house or flat which is let to three or more tenants who form two or more households and who share a kitchen, bathroom or toilet (see below for the definition of 'household'). In Scotland, the definition is three or more tenants who are not members of the same family or a member of one or other of two families. Accordingly, in Scotland, two households could be exempt if each household is a family. This applies equally to an entire house or flat and to a house converted into bedsits or other non-self-contained accommodation. Also, in Scotland, for a property to be an HMO the tenants only need to share one of the following basic amenities: toilet, personal washing facilities and facilities for the provision of cooked food.

- A house which has been converted entirely into bedsits or other non-self-contained accommodation and which is let to three or more tenants who form two or more households and who share a kitchen, bathroom or toilet facilities (see below for the meaning of 'self-contained accommodation').

- A converted house which contains one or more flats which are not wholly self-contained (i.e. the flat does not contain within it a kitchen, bathroom and toilet) and which is occupied by three or more tenants who form two or more households.

- A building which is converted entirely into self-contained flats if the conversion did not meet the standards of the 1991 Building Regulations and more than one-third of the flats are let on short-term tenancies.

- In Scotland, further classes of property can be added to the HMO definition provided that the basic requirement of having three or more occupiers forming more than two families is met. This might allow for parts of properties, or for properties where it was not the tenant's main residence, to be designated as HMOs.

In order to be an HMO the property must be used as the tenants' only or main residence and it should be used solely or mainly to house tenants. Properties let to students and migrant workers will be treated as their only or main residence and the same will apply to properties which are used as domestic refuges.

Self-contained accommodation: This is where the accommodation has inside it a kitchen (or cooking area), bathroom and toilet for the exclusive use of the household living there. If the occupiers need to leave the unit to gain access to any one of these amenities, the accommodation is not self-contained.

Households

The following are 'households' for the purposes of the Housing Act 2004 ('families' for the purposes of the Housing (Scotland) Act 2006):

Members of the same family living together including:

- couples married to each other or living together as husband and wife (or an equivalent same-sex relationship);

- relatives living together, including parents, grandparents, children (and step-children), grandchildren, brothers, sisters, uncles, aunts, nephews, nieces or cousins;

- half-relatives will be treated as full relatives. A foster child living with his foster parent is treated as living in the same household as his foster parent.

Any domestic staff are also included in the household if they are living rent-free in accommodation provided by the person for whom they are working. This does not apply in Scotland.

Therefore three friends sharing together are considered three households (in Scotland, 'families'). If a couple are sharing with a third person, that would consist of two households (in Scotland, two 'families'). If a family rents a property, that is a single household. If that family had an au pair to look after their children, that person would be included in their household. An au pair is not included within the definition of 'family' in the Housing (Scotland) Act 2006.

Exceptions

Certain types of properties are not classed as HMOs (and are not subject to licensing). These include:

- two-person flat shares;
- a property where the landlord and his household is resident with up to two lodgers (in Scotland, in addition to the resident landlord and his family there can be two other families);
- buildings which are already regulated, such as care homes, bail hostels, etc. (although domestic refuges are not exempt).

Purpose-built blocks of flats are not HMOs. However, if any of the individual flats are shared by more than two tenants in two or more households, they will be HMOs (in Scotland, three or more tenants in more than two families).

Houses which are converted entirely into self-contained flats will only be HMOs if the conversion did not meet the standard of the 1991 Building Regulations and more than one-third of the flats are let out on short-term tenancies. This does not apply in Scotland.

Licensing

At present, nationally, an HMO will need a licence if it is a building consisting of three or more storeys and is occupied by five or more tenants in two or more households.

If you think your HMO may need a licence, you should contact the local authority where your property is located as soon as possible and request an application form.

Even if your property does not come within the mandatory licensing category, it is still a good idea to check with your local authority (and go on their mailing list), as some may also license smaller HMOs, or may be considering introducing more extensive licensing schemes in the future, which may apply to your property. The London Borough of Newham for example now has a blanket licensing scheme which covers all rented properties, and other local authorities are considering doing the same. In Wales, a new housing bill is planned that will introduce a compulsory licensing scheme throughout Wales.

Note that the licence is per property not per landlord, and you will have to make a separate application for each property. If you sell the property, the new owner will have to apply to be the new manager as the licence is not transferable to a different person. Licences will normally (although not always) be for a period of five years. For more information, see https://goo.gl/MuvJpQ for England and http://goo.gl/w0awFi for Wales.

Scotland

In Scotland, the Housing (Scotland) Act 2006 came into force in August 2011 and sets out the licensing scheme for HMOs. Landlords should check with their local authority as to the rules that apply to HMOs. Some changes have been made to the HMO definition and licensing regime by the Private Rented Housing (Scotland) Act 2011; these primarily clarify the definition as opposed to changing it.

The owner of the property needs to apply to the local authority for a licence. The local authority can refuse to grant a licence if it does not consider that the applicant is a fit and proper person to hold a licence or if the owner or his agent is disqualified from holding a licence. A licence can also be refused if there is no planning consent for the HMO use or if the authority considers that allowing the HMO will result in too many HMOs being permitted in the area. If the owner/agent is not an individual, and a director or partner or person concerned in the management of the owner/agent's business is disqualified, then the local authority can also refuse to grant the licence. The local authority does not have to provide reasons for its refusal of a licence unless it is explicitly asked to do so.

Information regarding HMO licensing can be found on the Scottish Executive website at www.scotland.gov.uk/topics/housing. The Scottish Executive also provides a guide for landlords which can be obtained from the above website.

How to work out how many storeys there are

When counting the number of storeys in the building you need to include:

- basements and attics if they are occupied or have been converted for occupation by residents or if they are in use in connection with the occupation of the HMO by residents;

- any storeys which are occupied by you and your family if you are a resident landlord;

- all the storeys in residential occupation, even if they are self-contained;

- any business premises or storage space on the ground floor or any upper floor.

You do not need to count basements used for business or storage unless the basement is the only, or principal, entrance to the HMO from the street.

Temporary Exemption Notices ('TENs')

If you own a property which is currently operating as an HMO but you want to stop this, for example if you have just bought an HMO property but are looking to evict the tenants and use the property for something else, there is provision in the rules for you to apply to your local authority for a Temporary Exemption Notice ('TEN'). If this is granted, the HMO is then exempt from licensing and you will not commit the (criminal) offence of operating an HMO without a licence.

A local authority may only grant a TEN if it is satisfied that you are, or will shortly be, taking steps to ensure that the property will cease to be subject to licensing, for example if planning permission has been obtained for the conversion of the HMO to single family occupation.

A TEN can only be granted for a maximum period of three months, but in exceptional circumstances the local authority may issue a second TEN to last a further three months. No more than two consecutive TENs may be granted in succession for any property.

If the local authority refuses to grant a TEN, you can appeal to the Residential Property Tribunal, which can either uphold the decision or reverse it.

Criteria for granting an HMO licence

In order to grant a licence for an HMO a local housing authority has to be satisfied of the following:

- That the proposed licence holder (i.e. the landlord) and any manager of the property is a 'fit and proper person' (see below for further information).

- That the proposed licence holder is the most appropriate person to hold the licence.

- That proper management standards are being applied at the property.

- That the HMO is reasonably suitable, or can be made suitable, for occupation by the number of tenants to be allowed under the licence, with at least the minimum prescribed standards of amenities and facilities (see below for further information).

- Note, though, that some local authorities may impose additional conditions, which landlords will need to comply with in addition to the prescribed standards (described below).

The licensing application form will include questions which enable the local housing authority to decide whether or not the landlord and the property meet the criteria and can be given a licence. It is important that this is completed as fully and accurately as possible. Note that some local authorities are charging higher licence fees if the initial application is incomplete.

The local housing authority does not have to inspect the property before granting a licence, but in some cases an inspection may be necessary before it can be satisfied that the property is suitable for licensing.

Fit and proper persons

The application form will ask about details of:

- any unspent convictions for offences involving fraud or other dishonesty, or violence or drugs or any offence listed in Schedule 3 to the Sexual Offences Act 2003;

- any unlawful discrimination on grounds of sex, colour, race, ethnic or national origins or disability in, or in connection with, the carrying on of any business;

- any contravention of any provision of the law relating to housing or of landlord and tenant law (including any civil proceedings that resulted in a judgment).

Landlords who do not declare unspent convictions will be committing a criminal offence and will be subject to a fine of up to £5,000. There is also every likelihood that when this comes to light their licence will be denied or revoked.

However, simply because someone has an unspent conviction for one of these offences does not mean that he will automatically be denied a licence. Each application will have to be considered on its own merits, and the circumstances of an offence and its relevance to the licence application will be taken into account.

Amenity standards

There are basic prescribed standards for properties which are set out in the regulations, but individual local authorities can set higher standards. You will need to make enquiries of the relevant local authority for your property.

The basic standards (to which all properties have to comply) are as follows:

Kitchen facilities

- There must be either kitchen facilities in each room or a suitably located shared kitchen.

- Kitchens must have a sufficient number of sinks with hot and cold water and draining boards, installations or equipment for cooking food, electrical sockets, worktops, cupboards, refuse disposal and refrigerators.

- Shared kitchens must have adequate freezer space or a separate freezer and appropriate extractor fans, fire blankets and fire doors.

Washing facilities

- There must be either individual bathing and toilet facilities or shared facilities suitably located in relation to the living accommodation.

- For four or fewer occupiers there must be one bathroom with a bath or shower and one toilet which may be situated in the bathroom.

- For five or more occupiers, there must be one separate toilet with washbasin and at least one bathroom for every five occupiers.

Other amenity standards

- There must be the appropriate number and type of fire precaution facilities and equipment.

- Each unit of living accommodation must be equipped with adequate heating.

- All the bathrooms must be suitably and adequately heated and ventilated.

- Baths, showers and washbasins must have hot and cold running water.

- Bathrooms and kitchens must be of adequate size and layout.

Fees

Local authorities will charge a fee for licensing, which will be charged per property. There is no prescribed fee and it is up to individual local authorities how much they charge, save that the method of setting the fee must be fair and transparent.

Not surprisingly there is a wide variation in the fees charged by different authorities. The structures of the fees charged also vary; for example, some authorities are offering discounts to landlords who are members of local accreditation schemes, and are charging additional fees for incomplete applications which involve them in extra work.

Penalties

Failure to apply for a licence (where the property is a licensable HMO) is a criminal offence and can result in a fine of up to £20,000. Prosecutions will normally be brought by the local authority against defaulting landlords.

In certain cases, **rent from Housing Benefit or paid by tenants themselves can be reclaimed** if a landlord is found to be operating a licensable HMO without a licence.

Also, no Section 21 notice may be given in relation to a shorthold tenancy of a part of an unlicensed HMO so long as it remains such an HMO. This means that **unlicensed HMO landlords will be unable to evict their tenants by the notice only Section 21 procedure.**

Note that local authorities can also apply under the provisions of the Housing Act 2004 for a management order in respect of an unlicensed property, either as a temporary or as a final measure. However, it is unlikely that these powers will be used except as a last resort.

HMO licence register

The Housing Act 2004 requires local authorities to maintain a register of all HMO licences granted by them, all Temporary Exemption Notices, and all management orders which may be in force.

Registers will hold the following:

- The name and address of the licence holder/person.

- The name and address of the manager of the property (if different).

- The address can be a business address or a home address.

- The address and a short description of the licensed property.

- For HMOs, details of the number of storeys, shared amenities, the maximum number of occupants permitted, the number of rooms providing sleeping and living accommodation.

- A summary of the licence conditions.

- The commencement date and duration of the licence.

- A summary of any decisions of the Residential Property Tribunals in relation to the property.

The register will be open to inspection by members of the public.

The management of HMOs

All landlords or managers of HMOs need to comply with *The Management Standards Set Out in the Management of Houses in Multiple Occupation (England) Regulations 2006*. Note that these regulations apply to **all** HMOs, not just those which need to be licensed.

If you are not able to deal with the management requirements yourself, you will have to appoint a manager to do this for you. Ideally this should be someone who lives near the property as he may be called out at short notice if there is an emergency. The manager must be a 'fit and proper person' to manage properties (see above).

The regulations provide as follows:

- **Contact details.** The landlord or person managing the HMO (who will be referred to below as 'the manager') must ensure that his name, address and contact telephone number are made available to all tenants and are clearly displayed in a prominent position in the property.

- **Fire safety.** The manager must make sure that all means of escape from fire are kept free from obstruction and maintained in good order and repair. Any fire-fighting equipment must be kept in good working order and (unless there are four or fewer occupiers) notices indicating the location of means of escape from fire must be displayed in prominent positions so that they are clearly visible to the occupiers.

- **General safety.** The manager must take reasonable measures to protect occupiers from injury, with regard to the design of the HMO, its structural condition, and the number of occupiers. In particular, he must ensure that the roofs and balconies are safe or take measures to prevent access, and windows with low cills have bars or other safeguards.

- **Water supply.** The water supply and drainage system must be kept in good, clean and working condition. In particular, cisterns and tanks, which must be covered, and fittings must be protected from frost damage. The manager must not do anything to interfere with the supply of water or drainage.

- **Gas safety.** The gas regulations will apply as they do to all residential lettings, and the manager must supply a copy of the latest gas certificate to the local authority within seven days of receiving a written request.

- **Electrical safety.** Every electrical installation must be inspected and tested at least every five years by a qualified electrician and a certificate obtained. This must be supplied to the local authority within seven days of receipt of a written request. The manager must not do anything to interfere with the supply of electricity.

- **The common parts.** The manager must maintain the common parts of the HMO in good and clean decorative order, in a safe and working condition, and reasonably clear from obstruction. In particular, all handrails and banisters must be kept in good repair and additional ones added, if necessary, for safety; stair coverings must be kept securely fixed and in good repair; windows and other ventilation must be kept in good repair; there should be adequate light fittings; and all fixtures, fittings and appliances used in common by the occupiers must be kept in good and safe repair and in clean working order. However, this does not apply to items that the occupiers are entitled to remove (e.g. their own possessions).

> **Note**
>
> 'Common parts', for which the manager has responsibility, include entrance doors (including to occupiers' own rooms), stairs, passages and corridors, lobbies, entrances, balconies, porches and steps – basically, the parts of the property used by the occupiers to gain access to their own accommodation or any other part of the property shared by the occupiers.

- **Outside areas.** Outbuildings, yards and forecourts used by occupiers must be maintained in good repair, clean condition and good order, and gardens must be kept in a safe and tidy condition. Boundary walls, railings, fences, etc. must be kept in good and safe repair so that they are not a danger to the occupiers.

- **Unused areas.** If any part of the property is not in use, the manager needs to ensure that the areas directly giving access to it are kept clean and free from rubbish.

- **Living accommodation.** The manager must ensure that the living accommodation and furniture for occupiers' own use is in a clean condition at the start of the tenancy, and that the internal structure and any fixtures, fittings or appliances are maintained in good repair and clean working order, including windows. However, this does not apply to damage caused by the occupier failing to comply with the terms of his tenancy agreement or if he fails to conduct himself in a reasonable manner, or to things he is entitled to remove from the property (e.g. his own possessions).

- **Rubbish disposal.** The manager must ensure that suitable and sufficient litter bins and/or bags are provided, and to make arrangements for the disposal of rubbish with regard to the local authority's collection service.

> **Note**
>
> The standards of maintenance and repair required by these regulations will depend on the age, character and prospective life of the property and the locality in which it is situated. So, posh central London shared properties will need to be maintained to a higher level than tatty bedsits in run-down inner-city areas.

Tenants

Under the new regulations, it is not just the managers who have responsibilities. The regulations go on to say that occupiers must not hinder or frustrate the manager in the execution of his duties, must allow the manager access at reasonable times, provide the manager with any information that he may reasonably require, take care with and not damage anything the manager is bound to maintain under the regulations, deal with rubbish as required by the landlord, and comply with any reasonable instructions from the manager with regard to fire safety.

Any penalties for non-compliance under these regulations will apply not only to landlords but also to tenants/occupiers. However, in practice prosecutions are generally brought against landlords, not tenants.

Note

The provisions in the Housing Act 2004 providing for the local authority to take over the management of a property, referred to above in the context of licensing, can also be used if a property is not being managed properly.

Conclusion

What should you do if you think you have an HMO property?

- Contact the Housing Officer at the Environmental Health or Private Section Lettings Department at your local authority. It will advise you. If your HMO is one that needs to be licensed, you should ensure that your application is made as soon possible, and a licence obtained before any lettings are made.

- For the larger HMOs, you will need to check whether the property needs planning permission. If it does, then this must happen before any conversion work is done or any lettings made.

- Note that you will have to comply with the extra HMO management requirements (see above) as well as all the normal requirements (gas regulations, etc.) for non-HMO lettings.

- Even if your property does not need a licence right now, make sure that you are kept informed of developments as some local authorities may introduce licensing schemes for other types of HMO in the future, so try to be put on your local authority's mailing list. Many also have landlords' forums, which you should join. It is also a good idea to join your local landlords' association as it will keep you informed of developments in your area, or to join one of the online information services, such as the author's service at www.landlord law.co.uk.

CHAPTER 5

Finding a tenant

Letting agents

Using a letting agent is often a good idea. Sometimes it is essential, for example if the landlord is not local to the property. It is essential that there is someone local to the property whom the tenant can contact if there is a problem, and who can keep an eye on it and inspect it regularly. Even if the landlord does live locally, he may not have sufficient time to manage the property properly, in which case again it is best to use an agent. However, if the landlord can manage the property himself, the financial returns will be higher, as he will not have to pay the agent's commission. The larger houses in multiple occupation (HMOs) are best managed by the landlord personally as letting agents are rarely able to give the degree of supervision that this type of letting requires.

Agents will charge a fee and this will usually be by way of a commission. They normally offer two types of service. One of these will be an introduction service where they find a tenant and the landlord manages the property thereafter. Their commission here will usually be in the region of one month's rent. Normally, however, they will prefer landlords to use their full management service. Here, their fees will be in the region of ten to 15 per cent of rents collected. Usually agents will also charge extra for providing an inventory, tenancy agreements, overseas telephone calls and other special services. The cheapest agent is not necessarily the best – the fact that they are cheap may mean that they are unqualified, give staff no training, and don't pay professional association subscription fees.

When choosing an agent, be aware that there are no statutory or other requirements for becoming a letting agent and that anyone can set up shop if they wish. Be extremely careful in your choice, as there are a number of 'cowboy' firms around who provide a poor service. Remember that they will be looking after your valuable investment and a poor firm can cost you a lot of money. It is best to choose one which is a member of the National Approved Letting Scheme. This includes members of the Association of Residential Letting Agents (ARLA), the Royal Institute of Chartered Surveyors (RICS), and the National Association of Estate Agents (NAEA). If you use a member of one of these organisations, you can generally expect a higher standard of professional competence, a knowledge of the regulations, and fidelity bonding (a client money protection scheme). It is also a good sign if the agent is a member of the Property Ombudsman scheme, www.tpos.co.uk, and the SAFE agent scheme, www.safeagents.co.uk.

All letting agents are now required to be a member of a government-authorised property redress scheme. The three approved schemes are: The Property Ombudsman, Ombudsman Services Property and The Property Redress Scheme.

When choosing a letting agency, be aware that there is a great deal of variation between one firm and another, even among members of the National Approved Letting Scheme, and indeed between different offices of the same firm. Perhaps the most important thing is the calibre of the staff, their knowledge, training and general efficiency. When looking for an agent, ask around among friends and acquaintances, join a landlords' association and speak to other landlords about local agents at their meetings; speak to other landlords who have property with an agent you are thinking of using. Perhaps even pretend to be a prospective tenant to see how they behave. All other things being equal, it is wise to choose an agent who has been in the area a long time. They will usually have a greater depth of knowledge, and local knowledge is very important in this field.

A careful choice of agent is very important, particularly if you are going to be living abroad, as it is not unknown for agents to go out of business, which normally means that the landlord loses rent paid to the agent but not yet paid to him, and the deposit (assuming that the deposit is not held in a tenancy deposit scheme). This can put the landlord in financial difficulties if, for example, there are payments, such as mortgage payments, which need to be paid on the property, and he will be responsible for any returning deposits which are not protected in a statutory scheme, to the tenant. Also, the landlord will have to take over the management of the tenancy at what might be an extremely inconvenient moment.

A letting agent will almost invariably ask you to sign a management contract. Read this carefully. Make sure that it specifies that the agent will be responsible for carrying out the maintenance and safety check duties (e.g. regarding the Gas Regulations), and for keeping all associated records. The agent will also need authorisation to spend up to a specified sum on general repairs and maintenance. Check also that you are happy about all the clauses in the agreement, particularly those about termination of the agency agreement (sometimes a long notice period is specified) and about additional charges. If there is anything you do not understand, seek advice before signing.

Letting agents can deal with the preliminary aspects of evicting tenants (if necessary), such as writing letters and serving notices, but a legal representative authorised by the Solicitors Regulation Authority (SRA) must be instructed for any court proceedings. The agent can deal with this on your behalf if you wish, but the legal representative will need to a written authority from you confirming that the agent can give instructions on your behalf and liaise with the them on your behalf. Occasionally, agents will offer to deal with, for example, drafting and issuing legal proceedings on behalf of a landlord. This is not a good idea. The only people who can legally sign the court papers are the litigant himself or his legal representative (authorised by the SRA). An agent is not authorised to sign on a landlord's behalf. Note also that if the landlord is out of the country, it is essential that a legal representative in England, Wales or Scotland is instructed, as the court will refuse to make an order unless there is an address for service in this country.

Note

A District Judge informs me that a common reason for rejecting claims for possession proceedings is court papers signed by the letting agent!

If you are going to be resident abroad, it is usually a good idea to arrange for someone to have a power of attorney (either the letting agent, your solicitor, or a relative or trusted friend) so that if a problem arises while you are unavailable, someone is empowered to deal with it. However, unless you have absolute faith in that person, it is a good idea for the power of attorney to be limited (e.g. so he cannot sell the property and disappear with the proceeds!). A solicitor will be able to advise you and draft the power of attorney for you, or consult Lawpack's *Power of Attorney Kit.*

It is often a good idea for a new landlord to use a reputable agent to provide initial advice and to find the tenant, even if he wants to manage the property himself. An agent will be able to market the property at a suitable price and will have better contacts for finding a good tenant. Also, a good letting agent can often advise on small improvements to a property that can sometimes make all the difference in getting a tenant. Most letting agents nowadays will also have their own website where the property can be marketed.

Lastly, note that since 1 November 2013 all letting agents have had to comply with the Advertising Standards Authority requirement to show fees charged to tenants (such as for referencing), as well as obvious expenses such as rent. If you do not use an agent, you will also need to disclose these fees to tenants. The Consumer Rights Act 2015 imposes additional regulations on the transparency of letting agent fees, which need to be displayed prominently in offices and on websites; it also needs to be clear whether fees are per property or per tenant, and they must be shown inclusive of VAT. They must also state which property redress scheme they belong to and whether they carry client money protection insurance.

Note

Corporate tenants (i.e. large companies looking for properties for their staff) will normally only rent via a reputable professional agent (normally only members of ARLA or RICS). As these are usually excellent tenants, this is another good reason for using an agent.

Advertising for tenants

The following are some of the most common methods:

- **The internet.** This is probably now the most important method of advertising properties, particularly to students, as they almost always have free internet access via their university libraries. There are many commercial websites nowadays which will advertise properties to rent, sometimes for no charge. Landlords' associations also often have a website where members can advertise their properties, or if you are a large landlord, you could consider setting up your own website.

- **Newspapers and magazines.** Choose the paper most likely to be read by your target type of tenant. Usually this will be the local paper, most of which will have a particular day in the week when local property is advertised, and probably a property supplement. However, sometimes a different paper may be appropriate. For example, holiday cottages are often advertised in the Sunday papers or in glossy magazines. If your tenants generally come from a particular large company in your area, they may have an in-house journal in which you can advertise.

- **Shop windows.** This can be a cheap way of advertising a property if you are looking for a local tenant. Most newsagent shops offer this service.

- **Notice boards.** Perhaps the best example of this is university notice boards, if you wish to advertise properties for students. Be warned, however, that many student unions will only allow landlords who meet certain (often stringent) quality standards to advertise. Local businesses may, if you provide accommodation regularly for their staff, allow you to put a card on their notice board.

Consumer Protection from Unfair Trading Regulations 2008

On 1 October 2013, the Property Misdescriptions Act 1991 was repealed. Landlords are now bound by the Consumer Protection from Unfair Trading Regulations 2008 instead. These are policed by Trading Standards. Under these regulations, you must not only take care to be truthful in what say in your promotional material, but also be careful not to be misleading in what you leave out. So if the road is very noisy and you do not mention this at all, then you could be in breach.

For more information about this, have a word with your local Trading Standards Office. They will also usually have some helpful explanatory leaflets.

The paramount importance of a good tenant

Finding a good tenant is the single most important thing in letting a property (and good tenants can be worth a lot of money). If you have a good tenant, then any problems can be dealt with comparatively easily as the tenant will be reasonable about them (provided of course that you are, too). If you have a bad tenant, you will have nothing but trouble and may even end up out of pocket.

An example

A landlord lets to a 'hippy'-type family as he is anxious to have tenants in his empty property and the family say that they are desperate for accommodation. He is not entirely happy about them but feels that letting them in will be better than leaving the property empty. Once in, they proceed to redecorate the property, painting the walls black and all the radiators dark mauve. Numerous complaints are received from neighbours about their behaviour and loud music at night. There are several incidents when the police are called out and it is suspected that they are taking drugs. They pay one month's rent in advance but fail to pay any rent thereafter, and the landlord has to issue proceedings for possession to evict them. This process takes four months, by which time the rent arrears have risen to several thousand pounds. The night before the bailiff is due to come to evict them, they have a party, during the course of which several windows are broken, and other damage is done to the property. It is left in a filthy state with rubbish in all of the rooms. Much of the furniture has been either broken or stolen. The landlord is left with a property which needs several thousand pounds of work (including redecoration throughout and replacement of almost all the furniture) to make it fit for reletting, a bill from his solicitors for the eviction proceedings, and no chance of recovery from the tenants who have disappeared without trace.

This scenario is fictitious but all of the individual elements are drawn from the writer's own experience as a solicitor involved in evicting tenants. An experience as dire as this is rare; however, this does not mean that it will never happen to you. Be careful whom you let into your property. Once in, it is difficult and time-consuming to get tenants out, and there is little you can do, physically, to stop them damaging your property while they are in occupation.

By and large, there are many more good tenants 'out there' than bad. You need to develop techniques to ensure that the bad tenants in your properties are kept to a minimum.

Ideally, you will be looking for a tenant with a permanent job who will look after the property and will want to stay there for a long time. Long-term lets are preferable because this reduces the costs of letting and periods of time when the property is empty (when you will not be receiving rent).

A landlord says ...

'It is better to have a good tenant paying £500 per month than a bad tenant paying £550.'

References

The main types of references are employer's, bank, previous landlords' and character references.

The employer's reference is the most important as it gives some assurance that the tenant will be able to pay the rent. Remember that the applicant's current landlord's reference may not tell you the whole picture if the landlord is anxious for the tenant to leave, and character references can be unreliable (beware the reference which is too glowing – it is probably fictitious).

You should look for tenants with a good employment history. If the tenant has had frequent job changes in the past, this trend will probably continue, and he is less likely to stay in the property for any length of time.

References are particularly important for the more expensive properties, where they should be taken as a matter of course. However, for larger HMOs, many landlords do not take references and go by their own judgment. HMO tenants are usually in a hurry and are not prepared to wait for the time it would take for the landlord to obtain a reference. If there is any delay, they may well go elsewhere.

Note that when checking references it is best to take the approach that everything is fictitious until it is independently verified. After all, the person given as the employer could be a friend of the prospective tenant! You can often check contact details from the telephone directory or on the Internet.

A landlord says ...

'Do not trust fulsome character references – they are usually untrue.'

Credit reference agencies

These are usually fairly cheap and very useful; for example, they will pick up on the tenant who has County court judgments registered against him. Your landlords' association will usually be able to suggest a suitable company and many of the online landlord sites will also advertise credit reference agencies for landlords. If you are a member of a landlords' association, it may have a special arrangement with a company which will offer special rates to members.

If you have one of the special landlords' insurance policies, they also may be able to assist and have an associated company who can provide reports for their policyholders. Indeed, certain types of insurance, such as rent guarantee policies, are often conditional upon a good reference.

Tip

When doing a company let, check that it is a genuine company. You can do a basic company search for free on the Companies House website at www.companieshouse.gov.uk.

'Gut' feeling

This is often the best way of deciding whether a tenant will be suitable or not. It is a skill which develops with experience. Every landlord will have their own idiosyncrasies, and preferences and prejudices when choosing tenants. There follow some comments from experienced landlords on how they chose their tenants.

Never let a property to someone who comes to you desperate for immediate accommodation, particularly if it is late at night. These people will almost always turn out to be nightmare tenants.

A person with a cheerful, friendly disposition, and who has a sense of humour, is more likely to be a good tenant than someone who is grumpy and miserable.

Do not be prejudiced against Housing Benefit tenants. It is more important to consider the type of people they are.

A landlord says ...

'If in doubt, keep them out.'

Comments from HMO landlords:

> I never let to a tenant who is bigger and meaner looking than me.
>
> Beware of the tenant who, when you ask him where he is living at the moment, says, 'I am staying round a mates'.
>
> If people do not tell you where they are coming from or give you any personal information, don't let them in. There is almost always a problem past.
>
> I have generally found that foreigners and people from ethnic minorities make very good tenants. They are more respectful than many English people and usually would not dream of leaving a flat in a mess.
>
> Do not be prejudiced against a tenant's looks. Be aware of different cultures and age groups. Remember, con men are always well dressed and appear respectable.

Choosing a good tenant is particularly important for high-rental properties, as the inevitable delay in obtaining an eviction order may result in large losses. If a landlord is uncertain about the tenant's ability to pay the rent, he should take security in the form of a guarantee. However, careful checks should also be carried out against the guarantor, as there is no point in taking a guarantee from someone unless he is financially in a position to make good any losses caused by the tenant.

Tip

Be wary of letting tenants who take tenancy agreements away to get them signed by guarantors. It is not unknown for them to forge the guarantor's signature! Ensure that the guarantor signs in front of you or have the signature witnessed by someone you can trust.

It is sometimes possible to let property on a long-term basis to companies for housing asylum seekers. If you are interested in this, you can obtain further information from your local landlords' association. Many local

Sample tenant's letter of authority to Housing Benefit Office

John Smith
123 Any Street
Anytown
ANY 456

The Housing Benefit Office
Anytown Town Hall
Anyshire
ANY 123

Dear Sirs

Re: 456 Other Street, Anytown, ANY 789

I hereby authorise and request you to provide my landlord Arthur Rigby at 111 North Street, Anytown, ANY 999 any information he may request regarding my application for Housing Benefit and any other information he may request regarding my Housing Benefit entitlement and payment of Housing Benefit to me after my application has been processed. I also authorise you to provide details of previous applications for Housing Benefit if these are going to affect the rent paid to my current landlord.

I hereby request that Housing Benefit is paid direct to my landlord at 111 North Street, Anytown, ANY 999.

Yours faithfully

Signed ...*JJ Smith*............... Dated ...*14 June 2015*............
JOHN JAMES SMITH

authorities are now setting up schemes whereby they will lease a property for a period of years (often five) to use for housing homeless families. You will normally receive a rent which is slightly less than the market rate, but you are assured a regular rent for that period and the local authority is responsible for the maintenance of the property. Contact the Housing Officer of your local authority for more information.

Housing Benefit tenants

If a tenant is on benefit, he may be entitled to have all or part of his rent paid by Housing Benefit. There are many problems associated with Housing Benefit and many landlords have a policy of not letting to Housing Benefit tenants, although in some localities landlords will have little choice. However, provided you are careful when selecting tenants, they can be profitable and problem-free.

When a new Housing Benefit tenant is taken on, there is much that the landlord can do to help speed up the process. Housing Benefit Offices are often accused of unwarranted delays; however, these are sometimes because they are still missing some of the information they need before the application can be processed. It is important for your cash flow that payment is made to you as quickly as possible. Also, if there are long delays resulting in a large sum being sent to the tenant at a later stage, there is a great temptation for the tenant to spend it (rather than give it to you). The following points will help you:

- The application should go in well before the tenant is due to move into the property. Housing Benefit cannot normally be backdated to before an application is made.

- Under the verification framework, Housing Benefit Officers will need to see original documents. In particular, they will need to see the original tenancy agreement. Ensure that these are sent to the Housing Benefit Office promptly.

- Tenants should be asked to sign a letter of authority (see sample opposite) authorising the Housing Benefit Office to provide information to the landlord. If this is not done, the Housing Benefit Officers will not be able to give any information to the landlord about the progress of the tenant's application, even if they want to, because of the Data Protection Act.

- If you regularly let to Housing Benefit tenants, you may wish to consider keeping a stock of the claim forms to give them.

- Some tenants, particularly those who find writing difficult or whose first language is not English, may appreciate your help in filling in the application form. If you do this, you will at least have the security of knowing that the form has actually been completed and submitted! Remember, if you fill in the form for the tenant, you must state on the form that you have done this.

- If your property is an HMO, make sure that each individual unit can be identified (e.g. giving a room number). Try not to change these numbers as this can cause problems at the Housing Benefit Office and may cause it to stop payment of the benefit, if the change makes it appear as if the same room is being claimed for twice.

- Remember that Housing Benefit will be limited to the allowable rent for a unit of a suitable size for the applicant. For example, a single parent with a child needs a two-bedroomed property. If he claims in respect of a three-bedroomed property, he will normally only receive Housing Benefit to the value of a two-bedroomed property and will have to find the difference himself. This situation may lead to arrears building up. This should be borne in mind when renting to Housing Benefit tenants.

- It is possible for tenants to apply to the Rent Officer and ask him to advise in advance the rent figure that will be used as a starting point for working out their Housing Benefit entitlement.

All new applications for Housing Benefit made after April 2008 have been dealt with under the new Local Housing Allowance rules.

Tip

Ensure that the letter of authority that the tenant signs authorises the Benefit Office to discuss previous benefit claims with you, as well as the current claim.

Even if you and your tenant are meticulous in filing the correct documentation to the Benefit Office in good time, you may still experience very long delays before payment is made. The length of the delay varies across the country, but unfortunately in some areas it has reached a level which many landlords find unacceptable. If this is the case in your area, there is little you can do, other than refuse to take Housing Benefit tenants. New landlords and landlords buying property in a new area should make enquiries about this before accepting tenants on benefit. Your local landlords' association is a good source of information about this.

Housing Benefit claw-back

This paragraph will only now apply to those tenancies where Housing Benefit is paid direct to the landlord. There are considerably less of these with the introduction of Local Housing Allowance where the rent is mostly paid direct to the tenant.

However, if the rent is paid directly to you, one potential problem is that if the Housing Benefit Office discovers that an overpayment of benefit has been made to a previous landlord of the tenant, even in respect of a completely different property in another part of the country, it can deduct the overpayment from rent paid to the current landlord. It is difficult for a landlord to prevent this happening as, strictly speaking, Housing Benefit is a benefit due to the tenant, not the landlord, whose contractual relationship is with the tenant, not the Housing Benefit Office. There are several things landlords can do to protect themselves from Housing Benefit claw-back:

- Visit the property regularly so that you can advise the Benefit Office if the tenant has vacated or if there are any other changes in his circumstances that affect his Housing Benefit (so there will not be an overpayment to you).

- If you are concerned that there may have been a previous overpayment to the tenant, insist that the rent is paid to you by the tenant, rather than paid directly to you by the Benefit Office. The Benefit Office can only claw back from the landlord rent that has been paid to the landlord direct.

- Join your local landlords' association. Sometimes it has a protocol agreement regarding the circumstances in which a claw-back can be recovered from a landlord.

- If a claim is made against you for a claw-back, check that any paperwork served on you by the Benefit Office requesting a repayment is correct (if it is not, it may not be entitled to repayment). Your local landlords' association will be able to advise you here.

Note that under regulations which came into effect in October 2001, if a landlord reports (in writing) a suspected overpayment to the Housing Benefit Office, and it is found that the tenant has either made a fraudulent claim or has deliberately failed to report a change in circumstances, the overpayment will not now be claimed back from the landlord, provided the landlord has not colluded with the tenant in obtaining the overpayment.

Local Housing Allowance

Local Housing Allowance is a method of working out and paying Housing Benefit for private tenants. It is a flat-rate allowance based on the area in which the tenant lives and the size of their household. The Allowance will be paid direct to the tenant, and it will only be possible for it to be paid direct to the landlord or letting agent if the tenant is deemed to be 'vulnerable'. As now, the landlord can also ask for the benefit to be paid direct to him if the tenant is eight weeks or more in arrears.

Many landlords are concerned about the prohibition against rent being paid direct to them (except in the case of vulnerable tenants), believing this will result in tenants spending their rental money and accruing arrears. Here are some steps which can be taken by landlords to protect their position:

- Generally tenants will be classed as vulnerable if they are considered incapable of managing their affairs; for example, people with learning difficulties; some medical conditions; illiteracy or an inability to speak English; addiction to drugs, alcohol or gambling; people fleeing domestic violence; and people leaving prison. If any of these apply to your tenant, make sure that the local authority is informed as soon as possible, as it will take time for them to investigate this and make a decision. They will generally need evidence, such as medical reports, information about past rent arrears and the like.

- If your tenant falls into arrears, arrange to serve a Section 8 notice on the tenant citing the mandatory rent arrears ground as soon as the rent is technically in arrears of two months (see chapter 9). This will be the day after the second month's rent falls due (notwithstanding the fact that benefit is generally paid in arrears). Send a copy of the notice to the local authority informing them that you will be considering eviction proceedings if arrangements are not made to have the benefit paid to you direct; local authorities will not want the tenant to be made homeless and should therefore deal with this as a priority.

- Suggest to the tenant that he asks for benefit to be paid into a separate Credit Union account, kept solely for the Housing Benefit with an arrangement for the money to be paid to you by standing order. The account can be ring-fenced so that the money is kept just for rent and not used for other debts or absorbed into an existing overdraft. Note that the Housing Benefit Regulations 2006, Section 94(3) provide for the benefit to be paid to someone other than the entitled tenant, if the tenant requests this in writing. Further information about Credit Unions and how you can find one near you can be found at www.abcul.org.

A similar service to Credit Unions' is offered nationwide by Tasker Payment Services at www.taskerpaymentservices.co.uk.

'Bedroom tax'

This was introduced in 2013, with rules limiting the number of bedrooms that Housing Benefit will help pay for. Known officially as the 'under occupancy' rules, everyone else calls it 'bedroom tax'. It is an exceedingly unpopular rule and there have been many challenges in the courts. I am not going to deal with these here – for more on this see posts on the Nearly Legal Blog at www.nearlylegal.co.uk/blog. Be wary of letting to tenants where it is obvious that not all of the bedrooms will be used.

Working with the Benefit Office

Keep on good terms with your local Housing Benefit Office, particularly if you have several tenants who are on benefit. If you are considerate and helpful towards the Office, it is more likely to reciprocate. Remember also that the landlord has a duty to the Benefit Office, if rent is being paid directly, to keep it informed, in particular if the tenant vacates the property or is absent for a long period. You should also let the Officer know if you become aware of any other circumstances which may affect the benefit, such as the birth of a child, someone else moving into the property, or the tenant getting a job.

Valuation of benefit

Valuations used to be carried out by the Rent Service; it is now run by the Valuation Office Agency (VOA), www.voa.gov.uk.

Right to rent checks

These have been introduced to prevent people who do not have a legal 'right to rent' from renting private accommodation. After trials in the West Midlands, they are due to be rolled out throughout England from 1 February 2016. There are plans to extend them to the rest of the UK.

Landlords will be vulnerable to a civil penalty notice if they fail to:

- Check that prospective tenants have documents showing their the right to be in the UK.

- Make follow-up checks when a person's right to be in the UK expires during the tenancy, either when the right expires or after 12 months, whichever is the later.

- Make an official report to the Home Office if the follow-up check shows that the person no longer has the right to remain in the UK.

A landlord can employ an agent to carry out checks; if so, the agent will be liable to the charge, not the landlord. If you plan doing checks yourself, familiarise yourself with documentation provided by the Home Office, currently at https://goo.gl/0p0C1Z. Here are some important points:

- Check that people have a document which is on List A or List B (details online) and take steps to ensure it is genuine. You must do this in the presence of the person; it can be via live video link.

- In cases of doubt there is a government checking service you can use.

- These checks must be carried out on **all** adults who intend living at the property, not just the person signing the tenancy agreement (e.g. the wife if the agreement is just signed by the husband).

- Carry out the checks even if it appears that the person is English, otherwise, you will be guilty of discrimination.

- Keep records showing that the check has been carried out and a copy (paper or electronic) of the document(s), throughout the tenancy and for at least one year afterwards.

CHAPTER 6

The agreement

Why and when is it necessary?

Although there is currently no legal requirement to create a valid assured shorthold tenancy (AST) in England & Wales (although this may change in Wales after the Renting Homes (Wales) Bill becomes law), all landlords should ensure that their tenants have signed a written tenancy agreement prior to going into possession. However, do note that in Scotland it is necessary to have a written tenancy agreement for it to be a short assured tenancy (SAT).

Informal oral arrangements can be a recipe for disaster:

- If a tenancy is oral, there may be arguments later about its terms, even if these were clearly discussed when the tenant went in.

- Once a tenant is in occupation, you cannot then force him to sign an agreement that varies the terms of his tenancy, so it is essential that this is done before he goes in.

- The landlord will need a formal agreement so he can insert clauses that will protect his position (see below) and regulate the tenant's use of the property.

- If you intend to take a damage deposit which has to be protected under one of the statutory schemes, you will need to have a tenancy agreement.

- You will not be able to use the accelerated possession procedure (see chapter 9) to evict the tenant where there is no written tenancy agreement.

- If no written tenancy agreement is provided, a landlord is required by law to provide the tenant with written details of the main terms of his tenancy within six months, so he might as well provide a proper written tenancy agreement to begin with.

- Note also that Housing Benefit offices will require tenants claiming benefit to produce a signed tenancy agreement.

Although all tenancies should have a formal written tenancy agreement, this is not always essential with licences. For example, it may not always be necessary in the following circumstances:

- Letting a room in your house to lodgers.

- Bed-and-breakfast accommodation.

However, even if a formal letting agreement is not provided in these circumstances, there should always be some paperwork to prove the terms of the letting, in case there is a dispute at a later date.

A landlord says ...

'Do not let a tenant in until the paperwork is signed.'

Unfair terms in consumer contracts

These will be referred to in this book as the Unfair Terms Regulations. These regulations are the result of an EU directive which initially came into effect in July 1995; they were subsequently redrafted and the updated regulations came into effect on 1 October 1999. They are now part of the Consumer Rights Act 2015.

These regulations apply to all contracts which involve a 'consumer' (i.e. an individual not acting for the purposes of his business or profession) and a 'seller or supplier' (whose definition includes most landlords). They were designed to prevent consumers being placed at a disadvantage when signing formal contracts with large organisations, whose contracts normally include standard terms and conditions in small print. As everyone knows, these standard terms and conditions are rarely read by the consumer before signing the contract, and even if they are, he has no power to change them. The regulations provide that the consumer will not be bound by a standard term in such a contract if that term is 'unfair'.

These regulations apply to most tenancy agreements, as a landlord will generally be deemed to be acting in the course of a business. They will not apply to landlords who are simply letting their own home (e.g. during a year abroad) if they deal with the letting themselves; however, they will apply to all properties let through letting agents if the agent's standard form of tenancy agreement is used. They will not apply, though, to lettings to another business, for example company lets.

The regulations do not cover what are called 'core terms'. These are terms setting the price (i.e. the rent) and terms defining the subject matter of the contract (i.e. describing the property to be let). They may, however, apply to rent review clauses. A standard term is unfair if it creates a significant imbalance in the parties' rights and obligations under the contract, to the detriment of the consumer, and contrary to the requirement of good faith. The regulations are aimed at terms which have the effect of reducing the consumers' rights under the ordinary rules of contract or the general law. The regulations also require that plain and intelligible language is used and a term is open to challenge if it is difficult to understand by the ordinary person. The requirement of plain language applies to all terms, including core terms.

The fact that one term in an agreement has been found unfair does not affect the validity of the rest of the agreement. It is just that clause which will be unenforceable.

Consumers (or tenants) who have a complaint about a contract term can refer it to their local Trading Standards Office, which may in turn refer it to the Competition and Markets Authority (formerly the Office of Fair Trading). However, the main effect of an unfair term is that it is void and will not be enforced by a court in legal proceedings. So if rent is increased by a rent review term which is found to be unfair, a landlord will not be able to obtain a County court judgment in respect of the unpaid excess rent or obtain a possession order on the grounds of those rent arrears. He will also probably face an order to pay the tenant's legal costs.

In November 2001 the then Office of Fair Trading (OFT) issued a document called *Guidance on Unfair Terms in Tenancy Agreements* and in

September 2005 further guidance was issued. This advice (in particular the 2005 guidance) should be considered when drafting tenancy agreements. The documents can now be bought from the Competition and Markets Authority (which has replaced the OFT) or downloaded for free from its website at www.gov.uk. They are discussed in the sections below, where they are still referred to as the 'OFT guidance'.

It is, however, perhaps worth making a few general comments. Any clauses which limit or exclude rights which tenants would otherwise have had are almost certainly going to breach the regulations and be deemed unfair, unless there is a very good reason for them (which should be apparent from the agreement). Clauses which impose any penalty or charge on the tenant must provide that the charge be both reasonable in amount and reasonably incurred. Where a clause states that a tenant may only do something with the landlord's written consent, this should be followed by the words '(consent not to be unreasonably withheld)' or similar. Finally, any clauses which are difficult to understand or which use legal terminology which is not in common use, will also be vulnerable to being found invalid under the regulations.

Individual terms you will need in the agreement

Essential terms

Details of the following information **must** be provided by the landlord to the tenant whether there is a written tenancy agreement or not. It is a criminal offence for a landlord to fail to provide this information to a tenant within 28 days of a written request (unless he has a reasonable excuse, such as being on holiday).

The tenancy's commencement date

It is important that the tenancy is dated and that it is clear from the document the date on which the tenancy started. As set out in chapter 1, the law governing a tenancy depends upon when the tenancy was initially granted. For this reason you should always keep a copy of the first tenancy agreement, even if subsequent agreements are given to the tenant (although subsequent agreements should also be kept).

You will need to know the precise date the current or last fixed term started, for working out when the fixed term ends, and the days in the month or week when subsequent periodic tenancies begin and end. This information is necessary if you have to serve any Section 21 notices (Section 33 notices in Scotland). (For notices requiring possession, see chapter 9.)

The commencement date of a tenancy is also important for working out what day in the week or month the rent runs from. Normally rent is payable on the day of the month or week which is the anniversary of the commencement date (e.g. if the tenancy started on Monday 3 January, a monthly rent will fall due on the third day of every subsequent month and weekly rent will fall due every Monday).

Landlords who let several properties usually like all rent to be paid on the same day, usually the first of the month, and if so, the agreement should stipulate that rent is payable on that day. If this is not the first day of the tenancy, then the landlord has a choice. Either the rent is payable on a day which is not the anniversary – so for example if the tenancy starts on the 17th of the month then instead of being payable one month in advance it will be payable 17 days in arrears. Alternatively, the landlord could charge a smaller amount for the period between 17th and the last day of the month and stipulate that thereafter the rent be paid on the first day of the month and give a specific date for the ending of the fixed term, to be on the last day of the month. So, for example, the fixed term will not be for six months but for six months and whatever the irregular period of time was at the start,

The term

It is normal practice for a tenancy agreement to be for a fixed term, and the most common fixed term is six months. In Scotland, the tenancy agreement must be for at least six months to be a SAT. The legal effect of a fixed term is that you cannot evict the tenant (other than under the 'bad tenant' grounds – see chapter 9) and the tenant is liable for the rent, for its duration. So if in a six-month term the tenant moves out after four months, you can still claim the remaining two months' rent from him, unless you relet the property to someone else after he has gone or if you end the fixed term by agreement with the tenant. However, the OFT guidance considers that it is unfair to prevent a tenant from ending or assigning a tenancy if there is another suitable tenant available to take his place; see further on this below.

It is wise when letting to new tenants not to make the term too long. Tenants are not always as satisfactory as they seem when you initially interview them. For example, they may continually pay late, causing administration problems, or you may receive complaints about their behaviour from neighbours. If you have a six-month AST, you can simply serve a notice requiring possession on them to expire at the end of the six-month period and then if they fail to move out, you can evict them (see chapter 9). The tenants may object to this but there is nothing they can do about it. However, if you have given them a 12-month tenancy, you will have to wait until the end of the 12 months to get them out. If the tenants prove satisfactory, they can always stay on at the property at the end of the term, either under a new fixed-term agreement or under a periodic tenancy.

Another reason for going for a six-month tenancy is that in an AST the tenant has the right to refer the rent to the Rent Assessment Committee during the first six months. If the Committee decides to fix a new rent, this will apply to the whole of the fixed term, even if there is a rent review clause in the agreement.

Please see the comments in the commencement date section above on the length of the term where the tenancy agreement specifies that rent is to be paid on a day other than the anniversary day.

Note

Most local authority accreditation schemes provide for tenancies to be for a period of one year, particularly if your property is to be used to house homeless families referred to you by the local authority.

The rent

It is important that there is no dispute over the rent. The amount should clearly be stated in the agreement, together with the period of payment. It is generally best to make this monthly, as most people get paid monthly now. However, for some houses in multiple occupation (HMO) properties you may feel it best to collect rent weekly on the basis that the tenants are likely to be more able and willing to pay smaller weekly sums than larger monthly ones. You should in all agreements specify that the rent is payable in advance, otherwise the law will imply that it is payable in arrears. You can also set out in the agreement the method the rent is to be paid, for example by standing order into a specified bank account. For a discussion about when the date rent should be paid, see the paragraph on the commencement date above.

If rent is to be paid weekly, the landlord is required by law to provide the tenant with a rent book, available from Lawpack.

Note that there have been suggestions that if rent is paid in advance, this could in some circumstances be deemed to be a deposit, which would require protection under the tenancy deposit regulations (discussed later). Providing it is clear that the money is accepted as rent, and is credited to the rent account immediately, there should hopefully be no problem.

Tip

You should never allow a tenant the possession of a property until the payments for the first month's rent and the damage deposit have cleared through your bank. No exceptions should be made to this rule.

Other important terms

The following are other important terms, most of which should always be included in the agreement. However, unlike the terms above, you will not be potentially liable under criminal law if they are omitted.

A description of the property

This sounds obvious, but you should be careful to define the property accurately. If the tenancy agreement is for a room in a shared house, for example, make sure that all the rooms have names or numbers (and do not change them). Flats should be clearly described: first floor or ground floor, etc. – again it is a good idea to number them. You should also make it clear if any part of the property is excluded. For example, in a large property with outbuildings, some of these might be separately let as garages to neighbours or used to store your own property. The agreement should make it clear which of these are part of the letting and which are excluded. If the letting includes a parking space or garage, this should also be mentioned. This is particularly important for flats which all have their own parking space adjacent to the property (consider marking and numbering the parking bays).

Payments other than rent

The agreement should make it quite clear which payments will be made by the tenant and which by the landlord. For example:

- **Council Tax** – this will usually be payable by the tenant, but for HMOs it is payable by the landlord.

- **Water charges** – if there is no express provision, then they will be the tenant's responsibility. However, often the landlord will accept responsibility. Landlords should be wary of this though if the supply is metered.

- **Utilities** – for ASTs and assured tenancies (ATs), these are almost invariably paid by the tenant. However, in house-sharing arrangements, they may be paid by the landlord, particularly if he is a resident landlord.

For all payments where the landlord is responsible, the agreement should provide for the rent to be increased if the payments are increased, so the landlord is not out of pocket.

> **Tip**
>
> If utilities are to be in the tenant's name, it is best to arrange this before he moves in.

Penalty clauses

Tenancy agreements (particularly those drafted by some letting agents) sometimes include stringent penalty clauses, for example for late payment of rent. However, these are liable to be found void under the Unfair Terms Regulations and a landlord needs to be careful when using them. The following are examples of clauses that are often used:

- A clause providing for interest on late payment of rent. This is a standard clause. Unless the rate of interest is excessive, this will not fall foul of the regulations. Indeed, this type of clause is recommended, otherwise a landlord will only be able to claim interest on unpaid rent if he brings court proceedings. A typical clause of this type will provide for interest to be paid at one or two per cent above the bank base rate. Note that the agreement must state that interest is payable on rent 'lawfully due' or the clause may be invalid.

- A clause providing for a fixed penalty for non-payment of rent. If this is used instead of an interest clause and is for a modest sum, then it will probably be found to be fair, if challenged. A landlord could justifiably say that it was to make the agreement clearer and to get rid of complicated interest calculations. However, if it is in addition to an interest clause and/or is for a punitive amount (e.g. £15 per day), it will not be upheld.

- Clauses providing for fixed fees for administration expenses; for example, stating that charges of £X will be charged per occasion when rent is paid other than in the manner specified in the agreement (e.g. not by standing order); stating that £X will be charged every time the property is visited to collect or pursue late rent or every time a letter is sent demanding unpaid rent; stating that £X will be charged every time an appointment is missed. If these clauses reflect a genuine expense that the landlord will incur, then they may be reasonable. However, if they are in the nature of a penalty, they are vulnerable to challenge. For example, a 'missed appointments' clause would be fair if it provides for the landlord to pay a similar fee if he misses an appointment.

If it is important to the landlord that a clause of this nature (other than a standard clause for interest) is included in the tenancy agreement, it would be wise to specifically draw it to the attention of the tenant at the time he signs the agreement and explain it to him. If he agrees to it, you should ask him to initial the clause in the agreement. This would give the landlord some protection if the tenant subsequently challenges the clause.

Note

Any unusual clauses in the agreement should be given prominence (e.g. by having them in bold type).

The deposit

If a deposit is taken this should be referred to in the tenancy agreement. The wording of the clause will vary depending on whether the deposit is to be held in a government authorised tenancy deposit protection scheme (all tenancies given to assured shorthold tenants) or whether it is to be held by the landlord or agent, as in a common law tenancy. Common law tenancies occur where the landlord is a resident landlord, the tenant is a limited company, or where the rent is over £100,000 pa or under £250 pa (£1,000 in Greater London). For further information see chapter 1.

If you do not intend to take a deposit, then just cross out any clauses relating to this. Tenancy deposits are discussed in more detail in the next chapter.

Rent review

As set out in chapter 8, you can normally only increase the rent either by agreement (usually by the tenant signing a new tenancy agreement at an increased rent) or by serving a notice of increase. But a tenant may refuse to sign a new tenancy agreement and new rents in notices of increase can be referred to the Residential Property Tribunal. Rent usually cannot be increased at all during the fixed term. These potential problems can be overcome by including a clause providing for rent review in the tenancy agreement. It is important that this clause is as clear as possible and that any mechanism for calculating any new rent is easily understood and fair, to prevent the clause falling foul of the unfair terms in consumer contracts regulations.

There are different types of rent review clause. Some of them provide a mechanism for rent to be increased at specified periods by way of reference to a government index, such as the Retail Price Index. Others specify what the new rent will be, or provide for it to be referred to someone independent for review. Note that in the case of Bankway Properties Ltd v. Penfold-Dunsford, where a rent review clause in a tenancy agreement provided for the landlord to increase the rent substantially (from £4,680 pa to £25,000 pa), the Court of Appeal found that this clause was invalid, as it was merely a 'device' to allow the landlord to repossess the property (on the basis of rent arrears – the tenant could not pay the increased rent) and thus avoid the provisions of the Housing Act 1988; it was not a genuine provision for the increase of rent.

Most standard tenancy agreements, however, do not include rent review clauses, because if a tenancy is a short (e.g. six-month) AST, the landlord can simply serve a Section 21 notice (Section 33 notice in Scotland) and evict the tenant if he refuses to sign a new agreement at a higher rent.

Repairs and redecoration

Most landlords have statutory repairing obligations which they cannot contract out of (see chapters 3 and 8), but the agreement should state who is responsible for non-structural repairs and redecoration, which are not covered by statute. However, you will not wish your tenant to redecorate the property by painting all the walls black, so it is usual to include a clause either prohibiting him from doing any redecoration at all without the landlord's written permission (not to be unreasonably refused) or from redecorating in anything other than the existing style and colours. If the property includes a garden, the agreement should include a clause requiring the tenant to maintain it. Alternatively, you may wish the agreement to provide for access for your gardener (his charges to be included in the rent).

Note

All clauses forbidding a tenant to do something (e.g. redecorate) must be qualified by including after the prohibition the words 'without the written consent of the Landlord (which will not be withheld unreasonably)' or similar. This will prevent the clause from being invalid under the Unfair Terms Regulations.

Damage and alterations

The law prohibits tenants from deliberately damaging the property, and it is normal for this to be specifically set out in the agreement. Usually there are separate clauses relating to the property and its furniture. The law, however, does not prohibit 'improvements' and therefore the agreement should specifically prohibit any alterations to the property, unless the landlord's written consent is obtained in advance. It is also a good idea to include a separate clause prohibiting the tenant from changing the locks and authorising you to retain a set of keys (for access in the case of emergency).

Use

As the law allows a tenant to use the property for whatever purpose he wants, it is advisable to include a clause restricting use of the property to that of a single, private, residential dwelling, and to include clauses forbidding antisocial behaviour (i.e. causing a nuisance to other tenants and neighbours).

Note

It is inadvisable to formally agree (e.g. by a clause in the tenancy agreement) to allow your tenants to run a business from the property (however harmless it may appear) as if the business use becomes significant (and once permission has been granted you cannot prevent this from happening), this may result in the property becoming bound by the laws governing business premises. However, if the 'business' is in reality more of a hobby activity, this may well be something the tenant is entitled to do anyway and does not need special permission.

Access

The agreement should specify that the landlord (or his agent) should be permitted to enter and inspect the property upon giving reasonable notice in writing (say 48 hours) to the tenant, but it should also state that in cases of real emergency this requirement will not apply. This is important, as you will need access to carry out regular inspections, do any repairs and to have the annual gas safety checks done. Note, however, that you cannot enter the property if the tenant does not consent, even if you wish to enter for an authorised purpose (such as a gas safety check). If you do this, it can be deemed harassment, which is a criminal offence.

A refusal to allow his landlord access to inspect may put the tenant in breach of his tenancy agreement, however this of itself does not entitle the landlord to enter where permission has been refused.

A landlord says ...

'The worst thing about being a landlord is tenants ringing in the middle of the night because they have lost their keys.'

Assignment and subletting

Assignment is where ownership of the tenancy agreement as a whole is transferred from one person to another; subletting is where part or all of the property is let under a separate agreement.

It is essential that there are express covenants against assignment and subletting, as there is little point in carefully vetting your tenants if they can then assign or sublet to whoever they wish. In its guidance, the OFT, however, stated that it considered that an absolute prohibition against assignment could be unfair, as this could force the tenant to pay rent for a property which he may no longer need, for example if he has to move elsewhere for his job, even though there is someone willing to take the tenancy on. I take the view though that the OFT's point can be adequately met by allowing the tenant to end the tenancy early if a suitable replacement tenant can be found, provided the landlord's reasonable expenses are paid. The landlord can then grant a new tenancy to the suggested replacement tenant. This, to my mind, is a better solution than allowing assignment, which simply adds an extra layer of complication to the tenancy agreement. The landlord should be entitled to approve the new tenant, but the agreement should state that his approval should not be withheld unreasonably.

Insurance

The landlord will usually arrange for insurance cover, and the agreement should prohibit the tenant from activity which will affect the validity of the insurance cover and also provide for him to be responsible for any increase in the insurance premiums due to his behaviour. However, the tenant cannot be expected to be able to comply with this if he does not know what behaviour is prohibited by the insurers, so the agreement should also provide for the landlord to let the tenant have a copy of the insurance policy. Alternatively, he can provide the tenant with a summary of the relevant terms. The tenant will usually be responsible for the insurance of his own belongings. For more details about insurance, see chapter 3.

Note that any contract term requiring the tenant to take out insurance for his property, particularly if this is via a specified insurer, will be void. It is a matter for the tenant whether he wants to insure his possessions or not. You cannot insist upon it.

Tenants' property left behind

Tenants often go, leaving items at the property which can cause problems for the landlord. If the landlord throws away property which subsequently turns out to be of value, he may be subject to a claim from the tenant for damages. It is wise, therefore, to include a term in the agreement allowing the landlord to deal with of any items left at the property. However, this clause will need to be carefully drafted as the general law does not allow the landlord simply to take the tenant's belongings for himself or to dispose of them without notice to the tenant. For more information on this, see chapter 10.

Address for service

Under Section 48 of the Landlord and Tenant Act 1987, no rent is lawfully due from a tenant unless and until the landlord has given the tenant notice in writing of an address in England & Wales at which notices (including notices in proceedings) can be served on him. It is best that this notice is included in the tenancy agreement. The address can be the address of the landlord's agent or another contact address. This clause is particularly important for landlords who are resident abroad, which for this purpose includes those owners of property situated in England or Wales who live elsewhere in the UK.

In Scotland, the provision of the landlord or letting agent's details is required as part of the tenant information pack (see page 99), which must be given to the tenant at the start of the tenancy.

It is also a good idea to specify that any notices or other documents shall be deemed properly served on the tenant either by being left at the premises or by being sent there by registered post or recorded delivery.

Forfeiture

This is an essential clause, as it allows you to evict the tenant during the fixed term under certain circumstances (e.g. as specified in the Housing Act 1988 or the Housing (Scotland) Act 1988 in Scotland). The actual wording of most standard forfeiture clauses is somewhat misleading as it states that in certain specified circumstances (e.g. if rent is unpaid for 14 days) the landlord can re-enter and the tenancy will be 'determined' (ended). Of course, the landlord cannot physically re-enter the property himself: physical re-entry can only be done by a court bailiff (or Sheriff Officer in Scotland) pursuant to a possession order. This should be made clear as otherwise the clause may fall foul of the Unfair Terms Regulations. However, you should be careful about altering the wording of a forfeiture clause unless you know what you are doing, as you may alter its effect. A suitable form of wording for tenancies in England & Wales would be:

If the Tenant does not pay the rent (or any part) within 21 days of the due date (whether it has been formally demanded or not) or if the Tenant fails to comply with the Tenant's obligations under this Agreement, or if any of the circumstances mentioned in Grounds 2, 8 or 10 to 15 or 17 of Part II of Schedule 2, and in Schedule 2A, to the Housing Act 1988 arise, then the Landlord may, subject to any statutory provisions, recover possession of the Property and the tenancy will come to an end. The Landlord retains all his other rights in respect of the Tenant's obligations under this Agreement. Note – if anyone lives at the Property or if the tenancy is an assured tenancy under the Housing Act 1988, the Landlord cannot recover possession of the Property without a court order. This clause does not affect the Tenant's rights under the Protection from the Eviction Act 1977.

A suitable form of wording for tenancies in Scotland would be:

If the Tenant does not pay the rent (or any part) within 21 days of the due date (whether it has been formally demanded or not) or if the Tenant fails to comply with the Tenant's obligations under this Agreement, or if any of the circumstances mentioned in Grounds 2 and 8 of Part I and Grounds 11, 12, 13, 14, 15 or 16 of Part II of Schedule 5 to the Housing (Scotland) Act 1988 arise, then the Landlord may, subject to any statutory provisions, recover possession of the Property and the tenancy will come to an end. The Landlord retains all his other rights in respect of the Tenant's obligations under this Agreement. Note – if anyone lives at the Property or if the tenancy is an assured tenancy or short assured tenancy under the Housing (Scotland) Act 1988, the Landlord cannot recover possession of the Property without a court order. This clause does not affect the Tenant's rights under the Rent (Scotland) Act 1984.

If the tenancy agreement you are using does not state that the right of re-entry can only be pursuant to a court order, this should be added. This prevents the clause from being misleading.

Other prohibitions, etc.

There are a number of things landlords may not want the tenant to do, which can be set out in the agreement, for example:

- Keeping pets/animals at the property (although this clause must be qualified so as not to unfairly prevent tenants keeping harmless pets, such as goldfish).

- Using heaters which could be dangerous, such as oil or calor gas heaters (although do not just say 'inflammable materials', as this would be considered unfair as it can include a box of matches).

- Leaving rubbish and the tenant's own possessions in the property at the end of the tenancy.

Remember that you have no control over the tenant once he is in the property. The only way you can legally influence how he treats the property is through the tenancy agreement.

Unreasonable prohibitions and stipulations

It is perhaps worth mentioning here that although the landlord is entitled to include reasonable prohibitions and stipulations in the tenancy agreement, unreasonable attempts to control the tenants' behaviour while they are in the property will be deemed invalid under the Unfair Terms Regulations. For example, clauses that require excessive dusting and cleaning (I have seen agreements, for example, where tenants were required to clean kitchen surfaces with bleach after use and wipe down shower curtains) and clauses where tenants are forbidden to have guests overnight (the OFT guidance points out that this could cause difficulty if a daytime visitor fell ill). Other potentially unreasonable clauses are those forbidding moving the furniture, as this would include not moving the chairs.

I have also heard of instances where landlords (often elderly female landlords) regularly visit the property and order their tenants (often young student tenants) to clean and dust more frequently, as the condition of the property does not meet their own personal standards. This would almost certainly be deemed harassment of the tenants, which is a criminal offence, and a landlord who does this could be on the receiving end of a threatening letter from the local authority and even, potentially, a prosecution in the Magistrates' Court. As long as the tenant is not actually harming the fabric of the property, all you can reasonably ask for is that the property is left in a reasonable condition at the end of the tenancy.

Out-of-season holiday accommodation

This is where a property which is let out as a holiday home for part of the year (e.g. in the summer) is let as an ordinary residential letting during the winter months. Landlords of genuine holiday lets have an additional mandatory ground for possession available to them. However, for the ground to be available, the property must have been occupied for holiday purposes at some time during the 12 months prior to the granting of the tenancy and the letting must be for a fixed term of not more than eight months. The letting must be for a fixed term, not a periodic term, which means that a formal tenancy agreement is essential. A notice informing the tenant that this ground will apply must be served at the commencement of the tenancy.

The inventory/schedule of condition

If the property is let furnished, you should prepare a detailed inventory (often also known as a schedule of condition) of the contents which should be attached to the agreement. The inventory should also give details about items, for example whether they are new or damaged, and perhaps with electrical items the date when they were last checked. This will help prevent arguments later about their condition. Separate columns might be useful for items to be ticked at the end (and perhaps the start) of the tenancy. You should include the lampshades, curtains and carpets, plus details of the physical condition of the property, such as the walls, windows and doors, as these are also covered by the damage deposit. A schedule of condition should also be prepared for unfurnished properties, as this will provide evidence of the condition of the property (e.g. the walls, doors and carpets) at the start of the tenancy.

The inventory/schedule of condition should ideally be signed and dated by both landlord and tenant after an inspection of the property has been carried out. For more expensive properties with valuable contents, it is often worth taking photographs or even a video, as this can be used as evidence if a claim needs to be made against the tenants for damages at the end of the tenancy. Note that photographs must be very clear and include a ruler to show the scale. There are now phone apps which can be used to record a report on the condition of the property and its contents with photographs taken on the phone, and these may be worth investigating.

There are professional companies that can provide an inventory service, and these are often a good idea particularly for a first let or if you have a number of properties. They will of course charge for their services, but you can require the tenant to share this cost; for example, the tenant can pay for the check-in and the landlord pay for the check-out at the end of the tenancy. Note however that a requirement that the tenants bear all of this cost in the tenancy agreement will be void under the Unfair Contract Terms Regulations. When searching for an inventory company you should look for a firm which is a member of the Association of Independent Inventory Clerks. Your landlords' association should be able to advise you of any local firm or you can check the association website at www.aiic.uk.com.

In view of the tenancy deposit protection scheme, discussed in the next chapter, which applies to all new assured shorthold tenancy agreements, it is now even more important that a detailed inventory is provided and agreed by the tenant at the start of the tenancy. Bear in mind that it is likely that arbitrators in tenancy deposit disputes will place greater weight on evidence provided by an independent inventory clerk regarding damage to the property or its contents, as he is seen as being more independent and impartial. This is another reason why using an independent inventory clerk is to be recommended.

Guarantees

If you intend to have a guarantor, he can either sign the tenancy agreement itself, in which case it should contain a paragraph specifying the circumstances under which he will become liable, or he can sign a separate form of guarantee. You can purchase a *Rent Guarantee Agreement* from Lawpack at www.lawpack.co.uk. Remember that a guarantor will only be liable for terms that are brought to his attention at the time he signs the guarantee and not for any subsequent terms that may be agreed with the tenant. The guarantor should therefore sign a fresh form of guarantee every time a new agreement is signed by the tenant, particularly if the rent is increased.

Adjustments for disabled tenants

If you let to disabled tenants, be aware that under the disability legislation, you are required to respond reasonably to any requests they may make. The following adjustments will normally be considered reasonable, certainly so far as larger landlords are concerned, and should be complied with if possible:

- providing tenancy agreements in alternative formats, such as large print, Braille, audio tape, easy read;

- providing a British Sign Language interpreter during meetings with tenants who use British Sign Language;

- waiving a no pets policy for a disabled person with an assistance dog;
- spending extra time with tenants who have learning difficulties to make sure they understand their tenancy agreement and general rules, etc.

Stamp Duty Land Tax (SDLT)

This is a government tax (formerly just called 'stamp duty') payable on tenancy agreements, which is recorded by a stamp on the document. Since December 2003, very few new tenancies will now be liable for SDLT. However, SDLT was payable on many tenancy agreements in the past. It is important to note that if you are going to use them in court proceedings, a judge will not accept them as evidence if they have not been stamped. It is important, therefore, that tenancy agreements which are going to be used in possession proceedings are properly stamped, if SDLT is payable. Judges are now picking up on this point and it is most unwise to assume that they will not notice that the tenancy is unstamped.

Tip

Further information about Stamp Duty Land Tax can be obtained from the HM Revenue & Customs helpline (0845 603 0135).

Obtaining tenancy agreements

Lawpack produces excellent tenancy agreement forms for use in both England & Wales and in Scotland for a range of circumstances; see the example of Lawpack's *Furnished House and Flat Rental Agreement on an Assured Shorthold Tenancy* on the following pages or visit www.lawpack. co.uk. Landlords' associations often have forms of tenancy agreements available for their members, or forms can be purchased from law stationers, or on the internet (e.g. the writer's website at www.landlord law.co.uk). If you feel that any special terms are needed for your property, it is best to get a tenancy agreement drafted by a solicitor, rather than adapt one of the standard forms yourself, as it is easy to fall foul of the Unfair Terms Regulations if you do not know what you are doing. Be sure to use a solicitor who specialises in landlord and tenant work. Note that the author's service at www.landlordlaw.co.uk allows for tenancy agreements to be adapted if necessary.

If you let property regularly or you are a professional landlord, it is essential to get your standard tenancy agreement reviewed by a solicitor every few years, or to buy new forms. Changes in legislation mean that tenancy agreements that are perfectly valid one year can contain clauses which are invalid the next. For example, the effect of the regulations on unfair terms and the OFT's guidance has meant that almost all tenancy agreements current several years ago will now almost certainly contain a number of clauses which would be classed as 'unfair'. Plus all assured shorthold tenancy agreements have had to be amended to take account of the tenancy deposit scheme (discussed in the next chapter).

Tenant information packs – Scotland

In Scotland, all assured and short assured (SAT) tenancies which commence after 1 May 2013 require the provision of a tenant information pack to the tenant. Failure to provide a pack is a criminal offence punishable by a fine in the magistrates court. The pack must include a statement of the tenancy terms (usually the tenancy agreement), a copy of any AT5 notice served (required to create an SAT), a copy of the landlords gas safety certificate, and the specified tenant information pack document contained within the Tenant Information Packs (Assured Tenancies) (Scotland) Order 2013.

The landlord will need to sign a declaration that he has given the documents, and must also ask the tenant to sign the acknowledgement of receipt included in the pack. However, the tenant is not obliged to sign the acknowledgement. The regulations do not require a landlord to provide information twice, so if the AT5 or tenancy agreement has already been provided it does not need to be provided again as part of a formal information pack, provided the tenant has already given a written or electronic acknowledgement of the receipt of that document.

The information pack can be provided electronically if the tenant has previously agreed to receive it by electronic communication. In that case, the landlord must still get an acknowledgement of receipt from the tenant but it can be by way of an email rather than signing a form. Where there are joint tenants, the landlord must give each tenant their own copy of the gas safety record but he may then provide one pack to all the tenants. However, he must then obtain an acknowledgement from every tenant of the receipt; if he does not, then all tenants must be provided with their own information pack before the start of the tenancy.

Template tenant information packs are available from the Scottish government website, www.scotland.gov.uk.

Housing law reform

Tenancy agreements should reflect any changes in housing law and therefore landlords need to keep themselves informed.

When the Renting Homes (Wales) Bill – currently still going through the Welsh Assembly – is made law, landlords of property located in Wales will be required to provide tenancy agreements in a prescribed form to their tenants. This is not expected to come into force until 2016 at the earliest, and may be later.

Other documentation

There is an increasing number of documents that landlords now need to serve on tenants at the time the tenancy agreement is signed – here is a convenient place to list these, along with a few notes about each.

Section 21-related items

If you fail to serve these documens, you will be unable to serve a Section 21 notice:

- An Energy Performance Certificate (EPC).

- The gas safety certificate.

- The tenancy deposit prescribed information form.

- The governments *How to Rent* booklet.

The *How to Rent* booklet is only available online and can be found at https://goo.gl/kFDVba. The booklet can be served by email if the tenant consents; this means it should be sent as an attachment, rather than by just sending a link to the page where it can be downloaded. The government has indicated that it intends to amend this booklet regularly, so you need to be sure that you are serving the most recent version. If your tenancy is subsequently renewed, you will need to re-serve the booklet on the tenant if it has changed since the last one was served (but not otherwise).

Other notices

You may need to serve a notice on your tenants; for example:

- If you have a mortgage, your mortgage company may require you to serve a notice regarding its right to recover possession in certain circumstances

- If you have lived in the property yourself in the past or intend to do so in the future, you are advised to serve a 'ground 1' notice. This can be included in your tenancy agreement.

Other items

These will include:

- A detailed inventory – checked over with the tenants and signed by them to confirm agreement.

- Any other certificates (e.g. electrical – this may be needed for HMO properties).

- A standing order mandate.

- Letter of authority to the Housing Benefit office for HB tenants to sign.

- Manuals showing how appliances in the property work.

- A rent book, if rent is paid weekly.

CHAPTER 7

Tenancy deposits

A tenancy deposit is a sum of money taken by the landlord (or his agent) from the tenant at the start of the tenancy to provide a fund of money for the landlord to use after the tenant has vacated, should the property need repair work or should any of the items in the property need to be repaired or replaced. If the property is left in good condition, the tenancy deposit is returned to the tenant without deduction. Most landlords and letting agents like to take a tenancy deposit, as it is felt that this gives tenants an incentive to look after the property, as they will not recover their deposit unless they do so.

However, there have in the past been complaints from tenants' organisations that many landlords are not dealing responsibly with deposits. In 1998 the Citizens' Advice Bureaux published a report called 'Unsafe Deposits' claiming that thousands of tenants were being cheated out of their deposit money by unscrupulous landlords, and calling for a statutory tenancy deposit scheme similar to one which had been running very successfully in Australia. This was followed by a pilot tenancy deposit scheme which was run by the Independent Housing Ombudsman. Finally, provisions for a statutory tenancy deposit scheme were included in the Housing Act 2004, and these provisions came into force (in both England and Wales) on 6 April 2007. Further amendments were then made to the regulations by section 184 of the Localism Bill, which came into force on 6 April 2012. More amendments are expected to come into force in late 2014 or in 2015.

Tenancy deposit protection came into force in Scotland on 2 July 2012 under the Tenancy Deposit Schemes (Scotland) Regulations 2011. Turn to page 113 for information on deposit protection in Scotland.

However, the tenancy deposit protection rules do not apply to all English/Welsh tenancies.

The scheme currently applies to:

- all new assured shorthold tenancies where a deposit is taken after 6 April 2007; and

- all tenancies where a deposit was taken prior to 6 April 2007 but a new tenancy agreement is given to the tenant after that date.

The scheme does not currently apply to:

- tenancies which are not assured shorthold tenancies. These will mostly be 'common law' tenancies; for example, where there is a resident landlord; tenancies where the tenant is a limited company; and tenancies where the rent is over £100,000 per annum or under £250 per annum (£1,000 in Greater London). The scheme will also not apply to tenancies which are assured rather than assured shorthold tenancies;

- deposits taken for other types of occupation which are not tenancies, for example from lodgers

In this chapter we will first consider deposits where the schemes do not apply and the underlying law, and then look at the schemes in some detail.

Deposits where the schemes do not apply (i.e. tenancies which are not ASTs)

The tenancy agreement

In this situation you (or your agent) will be holding the deposit, and your tenancy agreement will need to set out how this will be dealt with. It is normal for the agreement to cover the following points:

- The amount of the deposit. It is usual for this to be the equivalent of one month's rent. It should not be for more than two months' rent, otherwise it will be held to be a premium, which is inadvisable.

- What the landlord can use the deposit for (e.g. damage to the premises or furniture, unpaid rent and services) and also any sum repayable to the local authority when Housing Benefit has been paid directly to the landlord.

- A requirement that a tenant should make up the deposit if the landlord has to use part of it during the tenancy (e.g. for repairs).

- Whether the tenant shall be entitled to interest on the deposit (normally the agreement provides that interest will not be paid).

- When the deposit is to be returned to the tenant – normally this is when the tenant gives up possession of the property; however, it is a good idea for the agreement to provide that if the tenant's Housing Benefit has been paid directly to the landlord, the landlord is entitled to hold the deposit until he is sure that there will be no clawback. He can, however, only retain the deposit for a reasonable period of time.

- The agreement should also state that the tenant is not entitled to withhold rent on the grounds that the landlord is holding a deposit. However, be warned that this will not always stop a tenant from leaving without paying his last month's rent!

Note

Most new tenancy agreements nowadays will be drafted on the basis that the tenancy is an assured shorthold tenancy and that the tenancy deposit scheme will apply. If you have a common law tenancy, you will need an agreement drafted for common law tenancies, available from www.lawpack.co.uk.

Fair wear and tear

When making deductions from the tenancy deposit, landlords are not allowed to claim for damage caused by 'fair wear and tear', i.e. damage due to the normal consequence of the tenant living in and using the property. Many landlords do not realise that they are not entitled to receive the property back in the same pristine condition at the end of the tenancy as it was at the start. The landlord is entitled to receive the property back in the condition you would reasonably expect it to be in after having been lived in for the period of the tenancy. If it was left in a clean and tidy condition the landlord is entitled to expect to receive it back in a clean and tidy condition, but he is not entitled to demand professional cleaning and redecoration. Note also that if a property has been let to a family with young children, the landlord cannot expect the property to be in the same condition it would be in if it had been let to, say, an elderly spinster. It is reasonable to expect that the property will have suffered more wear and tear with children in occupation.

Dealing with deposits during and at the end of the tenancy

There are often misunderstandings about the way deposits should be dealt with, particularly when proceedings are being brought for possession on the basis of rent arrears. While the tenant is in the property, the deposit is held by the landlord as security and should not be credited to the tenant against unpaid rent. When the tenant leaves, the landlord will inspect the property, and assess its condition. The tenancy deposit should then be used as follows:

- If there are any repairs that need to be done or items to be replaced, the cost of this will be deducted from the deposit. It may also be necessary to clean the property and again the costs of this will normally be deducted. It should be emphasised that costs must be reasonable and landlords should keep all receipts. There may be other deductions that are appropriate (e.g. if there has been a local authority clawback). However, all deductions from the deposit must be authorised by the relevant clause in the tenancy agreement.

- After these costs have been deducted, and only after this, the remaining money is credited to any rent arrears due.

- The balance (if any) is then paid to the tenant.

While the tenancy is continuing, strictly speaking the deposit should not be used until the tenants have left. However, many tenancy agreement clauses provide for the deposit to be used for any repair or similar work which falls due to be done (and which is not the landlords responsibility) during the tenancy, with the tenant then being asked to replace this money to bring the deposit up to the full amount.

At the end of the tenancy, the landlord should, ideally, inspect the property with the tenant (who will not be in arrears) the day the tenant leaves (the 'handover' meeting), the property will be in perfect condition, and the landlord will hand the deposit back there and then. If there are deductions that need to be made, the landlord should deal with any work quickly so as not to delay returning any remaining balance to the tenant. Often tenants will need this for the deposit on their next property and will suffer hardship if it is not returned promptly.

Tip

Make sure you use an agent who is a member of SafeAgent www.safeagents.co.uk. These will all have a clients' money protection scheme and you will not be at risk if the agent goes out of business. Otherwise, you may be responsible for paying the money back to the tenant yourself.

Tip

Many local authorities have tenancy deposit guarantee schemes or bonds to help people obtain housing in the private sector, who otherwise could not raise the initial payments.

Taking a deposit subject to the statutory schemes

All deposits paid in respect of assured shorthold tenancies must be protected under a government-authorised tenancy deposit scheme. If you take a deposit that is subject to the regulations, decide in advance which scheme you will be using, and make any necessary arrangements to join if required.

There are two types of scheme:

1 **Custodial scheme:** Here the landlord or agent has to pay the money over to the scheme administrators. This scheme is free of charge to landlords and agents, as the running cost is covered by the interest on the deposit money. There is only one custodial scheme which is called The Deposit Protection Service (DPS) – this is run by Computershare

Investment Services PLC. They are a large international company and previously ran a similar scheme in Australia. They have a website at www.depositprotection.com.

2 **Insurance schemes:** Here the landlord or agent keeps the deposit money, but informs the scheme administrators of the new tenancy. If the landlord fails unreasonably to return the money to the tenant at the end of the tenancy, money will be paid to the tenant by the scheme administrators. Landlords and agents have to pay to be a member of this type of scheme. There are the insurance-based schemes:

- **The Tenancy Deposit Scheme (TDS):** this is run by The Dispute Service Ltd which previously ran a similar voluntary scheme for regulated letting agents. The largest scheme is aimed at letting agents. However, more recently they have set up special schemes for landlords, in particular the Deposit Guard scheme which is run in collaboration with the Residential Landlords Association.

- **My Deposits:** this scheme is run in partnership between the National Landlords Association (the largest landlords' association) and Hamilton Fraser Insurance. The scheme is aimed mainly at private landlords, but it now also has a substantial agent membership. They have a website at www.mydeposits.co.uk.

- **The Deposit Protection Service:** the DPS now provide an insurance-based scheme as well as their free custodial scheme. See www.depositprotection.com.

All schemes provide a free arbitration service.

Which scheme should you use?

There has been a number of changes with the services provided by the various schemes. Originally My Deposits was the scheme aimed at landlords and TDS catered mainly for agents. However, now things have changed and all three companies provide schemes which are suitable for both landlords and letting agents.

The best thing to do is to visit all the websites, not forgetting the RLA's website which has information about the Deposit Guard scheme, and see which one suits your situation best.

However, the new Deposit Guard scheme is worth checking out particularly if you are a new landlord as this scheme provides a bit more support than some of the others.

TIP

If you are using an agent to manage your property, note that if the agent goes out of business taking the deposit money with him, this will not affect the tenants who will be repaid their deposit by the scheme. However if the agent used an insurance-based scheme, the scheme will expect the landlord to refund the money paid out to them (the schemes are there to protect tenants, not landlords). For this reason landlords are generally better protected if their agents use the DPS.

The tenancy agreement

It is essential that you have a tenancy agreement. If you do not, you will have little chance of success if your deductions are challenged at adjudication. It is the tenancy agreement which authorises you to make deductions from the tenant's money and says what the deductions can be for. So if you don't have a tenancy agreement, you don't have any legal right to make deductions from the deposit.

All tenancy agreements for assured shorthold tenancies in the shops will (or should) be suitable for use with the The Deposit Protection Service custodial scheme, and My Deposits insurance-based scheme. In the past, TDS required their members to put special clauses in their tenancy agreements, but this requirement has now been lifted. TDS now provide recommended clauses you can use, however you do not have to. Current Lawpack agreements are fully compliant with all schemes.

Note that as all disputes will be referred to arbitration it is particularly important that a detailed inventory is prepared and checked over with the tenant at the start of the tenancy. Indeed some of the scheme administrators have indicated that landlords will have little chance of successfully claiming damages from the deposit at arbitration if they are unable to prove the condition of the property at the start of the tenancy by way of an agreed inventory. Inventories are discussed in more detail in the previous chapter.

If the inventory was not signed by the tenant at the start of the tenancy, the adjudicator may be reluctant to accept your evidence, as they may consider it to be self-serving. For this reason, landlords managing their own property are strongly advised to use an independent inventory clerk.

How the schemes work

- Make sure, if you are using one of the insurance-based schemes, that you are aware of its charges, and that you have joined as a member.

- Within 30 days of receiving the deposit money you must provide the scheme administrators of the tenancy deposit scheme you are using, with such information about the tenancy as they may require. If you are using the custodial scheme you will also need to pay the deposit money over to the scheme administrators. The easiest way to do this is via the scheme website, which is totally secure.

- Within 30 days of taking the deposit from the tenant, you must give the tenant details of the tenancy deposit scheme being used, together with certain other prescribed information. You will find guidance on what you need to do from your scheme's website – they will normally provide a leaflet for you to serve on your tenants with information about the scheme, and also a form. For example, landlords using DPS will also find a form they can use in the landlords documents section of the DPS website. Otherwise, a suitable form is available from Lawpack or a similar form is available for members of the author's website at www.landlordlaw.co.uk. Note that if you fail to protect the deposit and serve the prescribed information within the 30-day deadline, penalties apply, so it is essential that this is done.

- During the tenancy you must comply with the terms and conditions of the scheme you are using. Make sure you have a copy of these and have read them carefully.

- At the end of the tenancy, you should check the property, preferably during a 'handover' meeting with the tenants. If possible you should try to agree any deductions to be made. If agreement can be reached, you should then, if you are using an insurance-based scheme, pay all or part of the deposit (as agreed between you) to the tenant, and inform the scheme administrators. If you are using the custodial scheme, the scheme administrators will need to be informed and they will then pay the money as agreed, within 10 days of receiving notification.

- If agreement is not possible, then you should inform the scheme administrators so the dispute can be referred to adjudication. If you are part of an insurance-based scheme you will be required to pay the money in dispute to the scheme administrators, and pay any undisputed part of the deposit to the tenant or keep it depending on what has been agreed with the tenants. If the money is held in a custodial scheme, the undisputed part of the deposit will be paid out as agreed between you and the tenant

- You and the tenant will both have to confirm that you agree to the dispute being dealt with by adjudication. It is possible to have any dispute resolved by the County court instead of by adjudication, but the adjudication procedure is so much quicker and simpler that most people will prefer it, particularly as it is free with no court fees.

- You and your tenant will need to provide details to the adjudicator to enable them to reach a decision. This will normally be done on the paperwork alone, without a hearing.

- The scheme administrators will pay out the deposit money as ordered by the court or by the adjudicator within 10 days of being notified on the decision.

Problems with the regulations

Tenancy deposit regulations have unfortunately been fraught with problems. Early legal cases made it necessary in 2011 to change the regulations via the Localism Act, which came into force in 2012. Now, the regulations have been amended again by the Deregulation Act 2015. Let's have a quick look at the problems that have occurred.

When is a payment a deposit and when is it rent?

This is the subject of the case of Johnson v. Old where Ms Old paid her rent six months in advance in respect of three tenancy agreement fixed terms before her tenancy was allowed to continue as a periodic. When the landlord tried to evict her under section 21, she claimed that the s21 notice was invalid because the three payments had been in the nature of a deposit rather than rent. The Court of Appeal disagreed and to the relief of landlords everywhere held that payments made in these circumstances will be rent and not a deposit.

Landlords should still be careful, as there may still be circumstances where payments taken in advance called rent, which are not credited to the rent account immediately, are held to be a deposit and subject to the regulations.

The need to serve the prescribed information

Many landlords have considered that the prescribed information is just a bit of bureaucratic nonsense and is not important. This was the view taken by the landlord in the case of Ayannuga v Swindells where he failed to provide all the prescribed information, thinking it unnecessary, as the information could easily be found online by the tenant. However, the Court of Appeal disagreed, saying that the prescribed information was of real importance, as it told tenants how they could seek to recover their money and how they could dispute deductions, without having to go to court. So the landlord lost his case for possession and was ordered to pay the penalty to the tenant.

The Deregulation Act 2015 amendments

The high profile case of Superstrike v. Rodrigues, highlighted tenancy deposit problems, which have been resolved by amendments to the tenancy deposit regulations in the Deregulation Act, which came into force on 26 March 2015:

- Where the deposit was paid to the landlord before April 2007 and the fixed term ended after that date, and the tenancy then ran on as a periodic tenancy, the landlord was under an obligation to protect the deposit at that stage and serve the prescribed information. This was the situation in the Superstrike case and which came as a big surprise to many landlords who had been advised that they did not need to protect the deposit in those circumstances.

  The Deregulation Act confirms that deposits do require protection in these circumstances, but landlords were given a grace period until 23 June 2015 to protect the deposits and serve the prescribed information out of time. Provided this was done, those landlords will be treated as if they had always been compliant.

- Where the deposit was paid to the landlord before April 2007 and the fixed term also ended before that date, landlords are under no obligation to protect the deposit and cannot be vulnerable to the penalty if they have not done so. However if they wish to take advantage of Section 21 to evict their tenants, they need to protect the deposit before a Section 21 notice is served, otherwise the notice will be unenforceable.

- If the deposit was paid to the landlord after 7 April 2015 and was protected and the prescribed information served on the tenant during the initial fixed term, the landlord is no longer required to re-serve the prescribed information if the tenancy continues under a new periodic or fixed term tenancy and the deposit continues to be protected.

- The Deregulation Act confirms that if the landlord's agent is dealing with protection of a deposit, the agent's name and details can appear in the prescribed information rather than those of the landlord, and this will not invalidate the notice.

Dealing with adjudication

The adjudicator will always deal with the case on the paperwork without any meeting, hearing or visit to the property. It is very important therefore that the paperwork you provide should be as full and helpful as possible. If possible the adjudicator should have:

- A copy of the current tenancy agreement.

- A copy of the inventory.

- Photographs to prove the condition of the property and its contents. Photographs must be very clear, not out of focus, preferably date stamped, and include a ruler to show the scale. Sometimes a video can be used, but again this must be clear and relevant.

- Any evidence you may have to prove that the sums claimed by the you are reasonable, such as estimates for work, and details of prices for contents such as printouts of details of similar items sold on the internet or the relevant pages of Argos or similar catalogues.

- A written statement setting out your reasons for making the claim and giving any other information you may think relevant.

- Any statements from others (preferably professional, independent people such as an inventory clerk, builder or surveyor) supporting your claim, and also from any (preferably) independent witness who can confirm the condition of the property. Statements should have the full name and professional qualifications (if any) of the person giving the statement, and be signed and dated at the end. Ideally they should also have at the end before the signature and date, the words 'I believe that the facts stated in this witness statement are true'.

Landlords should be aware that the starting point for any adjudication will be that the deposit money belongs to the tenant. Therefore, if the landlord is to successfully make a claim to this, he will need to show, by using the paperwork and other evidence submitted to the adjudicator, the following:

- that the damage or loss complained of actually took place;

- that it was caused by the tenants;

- that it is not something which would be classed as 'fair wear and tear';

- that it is not something the landlord is responsible for under either his repairing covenants or the terms of the tenancy agreement;

- that the sum claimed in compensation is a reasonable one.

In any legal case, one party will have what is known as 'the burden of proof', meaning that they are the ones who have something to prove. In tenancy deposit adjudications it is the landlord who has the burden of proof. The tenant does not have to prove anything. The money is his anyway.

Therefore, the quality of the evidence submitted to the adjudicator must be sufficient to convince him that 'on the balance of probabilities' the landlord's version of events is the true one, and that he is entitled to retain all or some of the deposit to cover his losses.

Many landlords have lost their case at arbitration, probably in circumstances where they should really have won, and have complained bitterly that 'the system' is weighted against landlords. In reality however, it is more often because they have not submitted their paperwork in time, and/or that the paperwork and other evidence submitted is not sufficient to satisfy the burden of proof.

Remember that this is a legal process where you have to prove everything on the evidence, and you should be all right.

Deposit protection in Scotland

Tenancy deposit protection came into force in Scotland on 2 July 2012 under the Tenancy Deposit Schemes (Scotland) Regulations 2011. This requires that deposits for all types of tenancy (not just short assured tenancies) in Scotland need to be placed into one of the approved protection schemes.

> **Note**
>
> Since 15 May 2013, the law has required that all tenancies in Scotland must have any tenancy deposit placed in a protection scheme, irrespective of when they began.

Currently, the three scheme operators are: the Letting Protection Service Scotland (www.lettingprotectionscotland.com); SafeDeposits Scotland (www.safedepositsscotland.com); and MyDeposits Scotland (www.mydepositsscotland.co.uk). Unlike in England, all the approved schemes are custodial schemes and none of them permits the landlord or agent to retain the deposit monies.

The Scottish regulations require that the deposit be paid into one of the approved schemes within 30 days of receipt. It is also necessary to give the tenant certain information prescribed by regulation 42 of the deposit regulations, for which template form is available as a download free of charge from the Lawpack website, www.lawpack.co.uk; alternatively, scheme providers may provide a document for you that serves this purpose.

Avoiding the tenancy deposit schemes

Many landlords are annoyed about the tenancy deposit scheme, which they consider to be an unnecessary bureaucratic burden upon them. Quite a few would like to avoid the scheme if they can. However, this is difficult and many of the so called solutions are not really satisfactory. Here are some of the ideas I have heard:

* **Taking a deposit which is not money.**
  This is specifically prohibited under the legislation in England and Wales and Scotland.

- **Letting property as an assured rather than an assured shorthold tenancy.**

  This is not advisable. If a property is let as an assured rather than an assured shorthold tenancy, then the landlord will not have recourse to the 'notice only' no-fault repossession procedure under section 21 of the Housing Act 1988. Although you may think at the time of letting that you will not need to evict the tenant, this view may change; for example, you may need to realise your capital to pay off debts or for an emergency, or the tenant may prove problematic, but not so problematic that eviction will be easy under the other grounds for possession. In both of these situations recovery of the property by using section 21 would have been relatively straightforward, but may be impossible if section 21 is not available. You could get stuck with a tenant you do not want, forever!

  In Scotland, this will not be effective as the deposit protection provisions apply to all tenancies.

- **Taking a guarantee rather than a deposit.**

  If the guarantee is under one of the local authority guarantee schemes, this is an excellent option. However, taking a guarantee from a relative or friend of the tenant is not really as satisfactory as a deposit; for example, if the tenant defaults on payment they may refuse to pay. You may be able to obtain a County court judgment against the guarantor but this will take time and if they have no assets, will be of little value. Even if they do have assets the County court enforcement procedure is very slow. Taking a guarantee is often a good idea if you are worried about the tenants' ability to pay rent, but this should be in addition to and not instead of a deposit.

- **Putting up the rent instead.**

  This might get around the problem, but it will also make your property more expensive and possibly less attractive to tenants (although of course they will not have to find a deposit). Plus if this brings the rent to above the market rent, the tenants have the right to challenge the rent this by referring to the Residential Property Tribunal, who may decide to reduce it. If this happens the landlord will not be allowed to increase the rent until after the end of the fixed term. Note that putting up the rent with a 'cash back promise' to the tenants if they leave the property in a good condition is not advisable as it would probably be deemed to be a deposit.

- **Insurance-based solutions.**

  A number of insurance companies are developing various options; for example, one company has a policy which will allow the landlord to claim for all damage done to the property (including malicious damage) under the insurance policy with just £100 deduction.

  Another solution provides for the tenants to be insured, with the benefit assigned to the landlord, for more than a the deposit would have been. However, this option is only available where tenants have a good credit history and these tenants are unlikely to be the ones which cause the problems.

- **Taking two months' rent, instead of one month's rent and a deposit.**

  This is not advised, as many judges will consider that the money is still a deposit, unless it is offset against the rent account immediately.

  As there is now no way that landlords can rectify the situation if they fail to protect the deposit within 30 days of receipt, this would leave you with no defence to a claim by your tenant to the penalty payment (discussed below).

- **No deposit.**

  If you have a good tenant and believe that they will not cause any damage, you may decide to take no deposit at all. This will be popular with the tenants and no doubt they will be pleased to learn that you are trusting them! However, you may get caught out if the property is left in poor condition when they leave.

Penalties for non-compliance

If you fail to protect a deposit which is supposed to be protected under the legislation within the 30-day time limit **and/or** if you fail to serve the prescribed information on the tenants, the following penalties will apply:

The tenant can apply to the County court for:

- repayment of the money; or

- an order that you pay the deposit money to the custodial scheme within 14 days; and

- an award of between one and three times the deposit money (the exact sum to be in the discretion of the Judge), to be paid to the tenant within one and 14 days.

Any Section 21 notice served will be invalid if a deposit has been taken and the requirements of the scheme have not been complied with. You will then only be able to serve a valid Section 21 Notice if:

- you refund the deposit money to the tenant (you will only be able to offset money due to you if the tenant specifically agrees to this); or

- if the tenant has made a claim for the penalty payment which has been resolved either by the tenant getting an order from the court of by the claim being settled.

Note that if you have protected the deposit but have failed to serve the prescribed information, you cannot serve a valid section 21 notice until after the prescribed information has been provided to the tenant.

Landlords are advised to keep an eye on the news and follow the various blogs and websites which provide news information for landlords, such as:

- the author's blog, the 'Landlord Law' blog at www.landlordlawblog.co.uk;

- the 'Nearly Legal' blog at www.nearlylegal.co.uk;

- industry news from Anthony Gold solicitors, at https://goo.gl/iaixUt;

- the National Landlords Association website at www.landlords.org.uk; and

- the Residential Landlords Association at www.rla.org.uk.

In Scotland, if the deposit is not protected and the required information is not given to the tenant within the required timescale, or at all, then the tenant is entitled to apply to the Sheriff Court. The Sheriff may order the landlord to pay the deposit into one of the protection schemes or order the provision of the prescribed information about the deposit to the tenant. The Sheriff may also order a penalty of up to three times the sum of the deposit to be paid by the landlord to the tenant. Further information about tenancy deposit protection in Scotland can be found on the Scottish government website at: www.gov.scot/Topics/Built-Environment/Housing/privaterent/government/SGTD1.

CHAPTER 8

During the tenancy

The covenant of quiet enjoyment

Every tenancy agreement contains what is called the 'covenant of quiet enjoyment'. This does not just mean that tenants are entitled to a noise-free environment, but that they have the right to live in the property undisturbed. This means not only that they have the right not to be illegally evicted, but also that the landlord should respect their rights and not do anything that will adversely affect their occupation of the property.

The covenant of quiet enjoyment is most commonly invoked to protect tenants whose landlord is trying to 'persuade' them to leave, perhaps because they are not paying the rent or because he wants the property back for his own uses, but is reluctant to go to court for a possession order. For example, such landlords may constantly visit the property, shout threats at the tenant, and interrupt the gas and electricity supply. This sort of behaviour is illegal and can attract both a criminal charge and make the landlord liable for civil proceedings for an injunction and/or damages.

However, the covenant for quiet enjoyment can also apply to other matters. For example, it can cover a landlord's failure to comply with his repairing covenants. The example given in the previous chapter of the elderly lady landlord visiting her tenants and ordering them to carry out excessive cleaning would also come under this heading.

It is important, therefore, that landlords ensure that they are complying with all their covenants, including their obligations to keep the property in proper repair (see below), and that they do not intrude on the tenant's privacy. These may conflict, as clearly the landlord will have to go to the property from time to time to carry out his inspections and repairing obligations. Some tenants may object to this and call it harassment (particularly if they are in arrears of rent).

If there is a problem of this nature or there is likely to be, then the landlord should take care only to attend at the property by appointment or by the invitation of the tenant. He should never use his keys to enter the property without the tenants' knowledge or permission, other than in cases of genuine emergency. If the tenant objects to the landlord attending to do inspections or carry out repairs, then the landlord cannot enter. This situation is rare, however, and if it occurs, then the landlord should consider whether he should bring proceedings for possession. Note that if the tenant's failure to allow access for repairs is causing the property to deteriorate, this may in itself be a ground for possession, but this should only be used (for the reasons given in chapter 9) if the deterioration is very serious and urgent remedial work is needed.

A landlord who treats his tenants with respect and who complies with his obligations under the tenancy will be protecting himself from any potential claims from his tenants. He will also find it easier to enforce his own rights against the tenants, should this be necessary.

Although a covenant of quiet enjoyment is not implied into licence agreements, licensees have the right to use the property for the purpose for which occupation was granted, which gives them a certain amount of similar protection for the duration of the licence agreement.

It is perhaps worth noting that if a tenant refuses to let you in to do repairs, he cannot then blame you for any losses he may suffer as a result of disrepair at the property, as it will be his fault that the repair work has not been carried out.

Rent matters

The rent book

If the rent is payable weekly, then a landlord has a legal obligation to provide a tenant with a rent book. This must contain certain prescribed information, but rent books can easily be bought at law stationers. Lawpack also produces one (see www.lawpack.co.uk). There is no legal requirement to provide a rent book if rent is paid monthly. Failure to provide a rent book will not prevent rent becoming due from the tenant, but technically the landlord may be rendering himself liable to prosecution (although in practice this is rarely done).

Collecting rent

In most tenancies the rent will be paid by the tenants by standing order. However, many houses in multiple occupation (HMO) tenants do not have bank accounts and will pay cash. For these types of tenants, often the only way the landlord can ensure that he gets paid is to go round and collect the rent personally. Collecting rent is a also good opportunity to inspect the property.

Good times to collect rent are either on Friday afternoons or Sunday mornings. Many people get paid on Friday so this is a good time to catch a tenant before he has had an opportunity to spend it. If a tenant is trying to avoid you, Sunday morning is the most inconvenient time for him to disappear.

Be careful, however, when collecting rent, that you do not lay yourself open to a charge of harassment. Be polite at all times, and never enter the property unless you are invited to do so by the tenant. If a tenant is in arrears, do not call round more frequently than normal (unless at the tenant's request). If the tenant makes a formal complaint about you, stop calling round altogether and make all future demands for rent in writing. You will also at this stage probably want to consider whether to start eviction proceedings – see chapter 9. If you think that the tenant is at all likely to make a claim against you for harassment, it is a good idea to keep a diary describing all contact with the tenant, giving dates and details of conversations.

Increasing the rent

If a tenant stays in a property for many years, the landlord will need to increase the rent from time to time. This can be done in one of the following ways:

For assured and assured shorthold tenancies

- By agreement with the tenant. This is usually done by granting the tenant a new fixed term agreement at a new rent. If the rent is increased by agreement, it cannot be subsequently challenged by the tenant. Note that if the rent is increased by agreement but not set out in a tenancy agreement, there should be some sort of documentary evidence of this, ideally a copy of a letter setting out the new rent and the date it is to commence, signed and dated by the tenant to indicate his consent.

- Pursuant to a rent review clause in the tenancy agreement. Again, if the terms of the rent review clause are followed properly, it is unlikely that the tenant will be able to challenge the new rent as he will be deemed to have agreed to it by signing the tenancy agreement in the first place (subject to the clause not being in breach of the Unfair Contract Terms Regulations).

- By serving a notice of increase. This has to be in the prescribed form, which can be purchased from law stationers (many of whom now sell forms via the internet). The new rent should take effect from the beginning of a new period of the tenancy, or after a minimum period of one month for a weekly tenancy. It cannot take effect during a fixed term, only during a periodic tenancy, i.e. after the fixed term has expired. A landlord can only increase the rent by notice once a year. If a tenant is unhappy with the new proposed rent, he can refer it to the Residential Property Tribunal (see below).

In Scotland, if the tenancy is a short assured tenancy, it would be better to bring the existing lease to an end by serving a notice to quit and a Section 33 notice and offering the tenant a new lease with a revised rent. If, however, the lease is an assured tenancy and the landlord has no grounds under the Housing (Scotland) Act 1988 to evict the tenant, the only legal way to increase the rent (failing agreement with the tenant) is to bring the contractual tenancy to an end by serving on the tenant a notice to quit. Thereafter, a notice is served on the tenant under Section 24(a) of the Housing (Scotland) Act 1988. The tenant must be given six months' notice of the increase of rent and if the tenant is unhappy, he can refer it to a Private Rented Housing Panel. Copies of the form can be obtained at www.scotland. gov.uk/housing/leaflets.

For Rent Act tenancies

Although this book has been written more for new landlords rather than Rent Act landlords (i.e. landlords of properties where tenancies pre-date 15 January 1989 in England & Wales or 2 January 1989 in Scotland), it is useful to consider Rent Act tenancies in this context. A Rent Act tenant has a right to apply to the Rent Officer to fix a 'fair rent', which is then registered and is the maximum rent the landlord is allowed to charge the tenant. The landlord can apply to have the fair rent reregistered every two years (three years in Scotland), or before this if the circumstances of the letting or the condition of the property have changed. Thus, if the property is substantially improved by the landlord, he can then apply to have the rent increased within the two-year period (three-year period in Scotland). Both parties can challenge the rent assessed by the Rent Officer by referring it to the local Residential Property Tribunal (in Scotland, a Private Rented Housing Panel). More information about this procedure can be found on the website of the Residential Property Tribunal at www.rpts.gov.uk.

Prior to 1989, fair rents were notoriously low and this was a disincentive for people to let property. Since the Housing Act 1988 (or the Housing (Scotland) Act 1988), landlords have been able to let properties at a market rent and this, together with the right to recover property under the shorthold ground, has meant that there are far more rented properties around. This, in turn, has had an effect on fair rents for Rent Act tenancies, as Rent Officers are now having to take these market rents into account when fixing the fair rent. As a result of this, Rent Act fair rents have increased, in some areas substantially, although there is now a 'cap' on the increase a Rent Officer can allow. This cap does not apply to first registration of a fair rent or where improvements or repairs to a property will increase the rent by more than 15 per cent.

If you are the owner of a property which has Rent Act tenants, you should bear this in mind when applying to have the fair rent increased – it might even be worthwhile taking some professional advice on the level of rent which is now achievable. Bear in mind that although the market rent is the starting point for Rent Officers in determining fair rents, they will then make deductions, for example if the tenant has carried out improvements, or if the property is in poor condition, or was originally let unfurnished.

As mentioned above, the Rent Officers' decision can be appealed to the Residential Property Tribunal (for more information see www.rpts.gov.uk).

Challenges to the rent – the Residential Property Tribunal

The Residential Property Tribunal has been renamed the First Tier Tribunal (Property Chamber) but we will still refer to it in this book as the Residential Property Tribunal. In certain circumstances an assured tenant can challenge the rent and ask the Tribunal to review it:

- For assured shorthold tenancies (ASTs) only, during the first six months of the tenancy. In Scotland, for short assured tenancies (SATs), at any time during the period of the tenancy.

- After a notice of increase of rent (see above) has been served on the tenant.

Unlike Rent Act tenancies, the tenant cannot refer the rent to the Rent Officer and his only role with ATs and ASTs is assessing rents for the purpose of Housing Benefit payments.

When a rent is referred to the Residential Property Tribunal it will then notify the other party and both parties will be asked to make written representations. The rent can be either considered on the written representations alone or either party can request a hearing.

The application will be considered by a panel drawn from the committee's members. Panel members can either be lawyers, valuers or lay members. There is always a valuer on every committee, and the valuer will be one who has good local knowledge of the area where the property is situated. For a hearing, the panel will normally consist of three members; for considering written representations, it may be only two.

Even if there is going to be a hearing, written representations and evidence should be sent to the panel **at least seven days** before the hearing. This is because the rules require copies to be served on the other side so the panel can be given a reasonable opportunity to consider it. If evidence is provided too close to the hearing date, you will risk having the hearing adjourned, particularly if the tenant does not attend the hearing.

What the panel has to consider is (in the case of ASTs only):

1. Is there a sufficient number of dwellings let on ATs in the area for the panel to be able to do a comparison? If yes, then:

2. Is the rent significantly higher than the level of rents in the locality (i.e. more than about five to ten per cent)? If yes, then:

3. What is the market rent for this tenancy? And:

4. From what date should any new rent start?

For ATs (not shortholds), the panel only has to consider questions 3 and 4.

The following points may assist you if you have had a property referred to the Residential Property Tribunal:

- Bear in mind that the panel will always inspect the property, so make sure it is in good condition.

- The panel will not take future works into account when assessing the rent (i.e. it will not assess a higher rent because you have planned substantial improvements).

- If improvements/repairs are being done at the property, the landlord can (and should) ask the committee to adjourn the assessment until they are completed (because the assessed rent will probably be low if the inspection takes place while works are being carried out).

- The panel will disregard the effect of any improvements made by the tenant, any deterioration in the property caused by the tenant, and the effect of any service charges for which the landlord is responsible. Thus, the tenant will not be penalised by having his rent increased because he has carried out improvements, neither can he take advantage of his own neglect of the property by being able to claim a lower rent.

- The panel cannot take the personal circumstances of either the landlord or the tenant into account – its job is to determine the market rent.

- Evidence of the rental of lettings of a similar type in the locality (e.g. in the same street) will be very useful to the panel – it will need to know the type of tenancy, its terms, the size of the property let, the rent and what is included in the letting (e.g. if it is furnished or unfurnished, and if furnished, what is included).

- The panel will take particular note of very recent lettings, bearing in mind that the market can fluctuate over a short period.

- Advertisements for rented properties in the local paper will be of limited value, as the panel will have no evidence that these properties will actually achieve a tenant at the advertised rent.

- Bear in mind that a house will achieve a higher rental value overall if let on a room-by-room basis, with each tenant having his own tenancy agreement, as opposed to being let as one property under one tenancy agreement with all tenants having joint and several liability for the whole of the rent.

Once the panel has made its decision, it will provide both parties with a decision sheet. It will also give a statement of its reasons for coming to its decision. There is a right of appeal from the panel's decision to the High Court, and from there to the Court of Appeal. However, you can only appeal the panel's decision on the basis that it has wrongly interpreted the law, not because you disagree with the way that it has interpreted the facts. This procedure is, of course, expensive and time-consuming and it unlikely to be followed by the small landlord.

If you are unhappy with the administration of panel cases, you can complain to the Parliamentary Ombudsman. However, he will not look at the actual decision reached by the panel, just the procedures that were used to reach that decision.

Further information about the Residential Property Tribunal and its work can be obtained from its website at www.gov.uk/housing-tribunals.

In Scotland, the Residential Property Tribunal has been replaced by the Private Rented Housing Panel; the procedure is broadly similar to that of the Residential Property Tribunal. Further details can be obtained from the Private Rented Housing Panel website at www.prhpscotland.gov.uk or a guide can be obtained from the Private Rented Housing Panel offices.

Repairing duties/access

All landlords have the right to obtain access to the property to inspect its condition, but, other than in cases of extreme emergency, this must not be without the tenant's knowledge and consent. Unauthorised access by the landlord may be deemed as trespass and he may also fall foul of the harassment legislation. See the discussion above at the start of this chapter regarding the covenant of quiet enjoyment.

It is important that the property is maintained in good repair throughout the tenancy (or at least those parts for which the landlord has responsibility).

If it is not, the tenant will be able to bring proceedings in the County court (or Sheriff Court in Scotland) for a court order compelling the landlord to do the repairs, or he may be entitled to do the work himself and deduct the (reasonable) cost from the rent. Note that if the tenant wishes to bring proceedings based on disrepair, he will now have to comply with the County courts Pre-Action Protocol for Housing Disrepair cases, which came into force on 8 December 2003 (this does not apply in Scotland). This sets out the procedure which the tenant has to follow before starting a court action, which includes sending a letter to the landlord providing full details of the disrepair complained of. A copy of the Protocol can be downloaded from the Court Service website at http://hmctsformfinder.justice.gov.uk.

In Scotland, the 2006 Act allows a tenant to apply to the Private Rented Housing Panel (PRHP) if the tenant considers the landlord has failed to comply with his obligations to keep the property in good repair. The Private Rented Housing Panel has the power to make an order (called a repairing standard enforcement order) requiring the landlord to carry out any necessary work within a specified period. If the landlord fails to comply the Private Rented Housing Panel serves notice on the local authority. The local authority can grant a rent relief order which can reduce the rent payable on the property by up to 90 per cent until the work has been completed. It is also a criminal offence to fail to comply with a repairing standard enforcement order without reasonable excuse; the penalty is a fine. Once the provisions of the current Housing (Scotland) Bill are brought into force, the local authority will also be entitled to make an application to the PRHP if the tenant is unwilling to do so.

The tenant will also be able to use the fact of the disrepair to defend any legal proceedings the landlord may bring, for example to obtain a possession order on the grounds of rent arrears. In this case, he will not need to comply with the Pre-Action Protocol.

The tenant, if financially eligible, may be able to obtain Legal Aid. If he is successful in any legal proceedings, the landlord will also normally be ordered to pay the tenant's legal costs, which could be substantial. It is important therefore that action is taken promptly if a letter regarding disrepair is received from the tenant or from his solicitor, assuming of course that the allegations are well founded.

As well as going to court, a tenant can also complain about the condition of the property to the Housing Officer in the environmental health department of his local authority, who will normally then attend and inspect the property. If the property is shown to have any Category 1 hazards, then the local authority will have to serve an improvement notice on the landlord. For more information about this, see the section on local authority powers in chapter 3.

It is important therefore that all complaints by tenants are dealt with promptly and that the property is regularly inspected and repairs carried out as necessary. However, a landlord cannot normally be required by a tenant to improve a property (unless it falls short of the basic standards); for example, a tenant cannot insist on normal windows being double-glazed. Also, the legislation provides that the character and prospective life-span of a property and the locality in which it is situated will affect the standard of repair required. The standard will therefore be different for quality housing in a 'good' neighbourhood, than for poor housing in a run-down district.

Prosecutions under the Environmental Protection Act 1990

If a property is in such a state of disrepair that it is considered to be a public nuisance, it may be possible for tenants to bring a prosecution under the Environmental Protection Act. My Landlord-Law Blog records several instances of successful prosecutions bring brought against a local authority where a property was suffering from severe damp and condensation. The same procedure can also be used against landlords in the private sector. If a landlord is found guilty, the court can order the landlord to carry out remedial work (including works to improve the property that he would not be liable for under the statutory repairing covenants) and also compensation for the tenant. The process involves serving a formal notice on the landlord and then waiting 21 days before commencing court action. Landlords served with council or tenant notices about damp and mould should act quickly and obtain specialist advice.

Tip

If a landlord has an obligation to repair or the right to enter and repair (which is usual), then he may be liable to a passer-by or an adjoining owner if damage is caused, **even if he does not know of the problem.**

HMO properties

If you are an HMO landlord, you will, in addition to the above, need to comply with the management standards, further details of which are set out in chapter 4. Note that all HMO landlords will have to comply with these, not just landlords of HMO properties which need to be licensed.

It is a good idea to inspect the larger HMO properties more frequently than is the case (or indeed advisable bearing in mind that you do not want to be accused of harassment) with the smaller properties, particularly those larger HMOs with a large number of individual tenants. Often these will need to be checked and visited at least once a week to ensure that minor problems do not escalate into major ones.

Anti-retaliatory eviction rules

These are new rules were introduced by section 33 of the Deregulation Act 2015. They aim to stop situations where landlords decide to evict tenants under Section 21, if the tenants complain about the poor standard of the property during the tenancy.

The rules provide that landlords cannot serve a valid Section 21 notice within 6 months of service by the local authority of one of three notices:

1 a notice served under section 11 of the Housing Act 2004 (improvement notices relating to category 1 hazards);

2 a notice served under section 12 of that Act (improvement notices relating to category 2 hazards); or

3 a notice served under section 40(7) of that Act (emergency remedial action).

The notices will be served on the landlord if a Housing Health and Safety Rating System inspection (discussed in chapter 3) is done at the property and the inspection shows the property has a category 1 or category 2 hazard.

The only way a landlord will be able to serve a valid Section 21 is if the local authority agrees to suspend the notice – which they will only do if you are either able to show that the notice should not have been served in the first place, or if the work is done.

The rules also provide for a Section 21 notice served after a complaint is made by the tenant to retrospectively become invalid if the local authority subsequently serves one of the three notices listed above, for the same, or substantially the same, issues.

If a tenant makes a complaint to you about the property, the Act states that landlords need to respond 'adequately'. This means that you must:

- provide a description of the action you intend to take to address the complaint; and

- set out a reasonable timescale for taking this action.

It is not clear from the legislation however whether doing this will affect whether or not your Section 21 notice is retrospectively invalidated by the service of a local authority notice. The best advice for landlords is to comply and then to get the work done as soon as possible.

Note that landlords whose property is in good condition should not fear this legislation, as local authority Environmental Health Officers are not going to serve notices for trivial matters.

Note also that the rules will not apply if tenants have done the damage themselves. This means that having a detailed inventory taken at the start of the tenancy is very important, as this will be your proof that the property was in good condition when let to tenants.

There is a further exemption if the property is genuinely on the market for sale. However, the exemption will not apply if the property is sold to an associate or business partner of the landlord (which includes employees).

Housing Benefit

You will need to keep an eye on the property and inform the Benefit Office if the tenant vacates or if his circumstances change. Keep a record of when the tenant needs to reapply for benefit and make sure that he does so.

New tenancy agreements

When a fixed term comes to an end, you may wish to grant the tenant a new fixed term. It is a good idea to do this, as you can then use this as a method of increasing the rent (see 'Rent matters' above). You can also incorporate new terms in the agreement. You may wish to do this as a result of new legislation, or to protect yourself against a problem you have encountered. If you have a number of rented properties, it is a good idea to have a standard tenancy agreement which you review from time to time to take account of these matters.

Lawpack tenancy agreements are periodically reviewed and updated to take account of legislation as are those on the authors website at www.landlordlaw.co.uk. Landlords' associations will also periodically review their agreements. It is best, therefore, to buy new agreements rather than just photocopying an old agreement which may be out of date. For example, tenancy agreements had to be reviewed after the Office of Fair Trading issued fresh guidance on unfair terms in September 2005.

Landlords should note, however, that it is not essential to give the tenant a new form of fixed term tenancy agreement on expiry of the old one. A tenancy agreement will automatically continue on a 'periodic' basis, from month to month if rent is paid monthly, or from week to week if the rent is paid weekly, under the same terms and conditions as the original 'fixed term' tenancy. Many tenants have continued to live in their properties for years under periodic tenancies. Indeed, a periodic tenancy is sometimes preferable as it gives more flexibility, for example if the landlord thinks he may wish to recover his property but is not sure when, or if the tenant thinks he may need to move out (e.g. if he is likely to be relocated) during the next few months. Many agents insist on providing new tenancy agreements (and of course making a charge for this service) and this often gives the impression that a new fixed term agreement is essential; however, this is not the case.

In Scotland, if a new tenancy agreement is not provided, the tenancy continues on the same terms and conditions and for the same period as the original lease, unless the tenancy agreement specifically provides that after the initial fixed term (which must be for a period of at least six months) the lease can continue for a further shorter period (e.g. on a month-to-month basis thereafter). It does not therefore offer the same flexibility as a periodic tenancy in England & Wales.

Note also that a landlord cannot force a tenant to sign a new agreement if he does not want to. However, under an AST, if a tenant refuses to sign, the landlord always has the option of serving a notice seeking possession and thereafter repossessing the property if the tenant refuses to sign a new agreement, for example with an increased rent. However, if the tenancy is an AT where the shorthold/notice only ground for possession is not available or a Rent Act tenancy, the tenant will often be advised not to sign a new tenancy agreement, for example if it contains more onerous terms. There is a procedure whereby landlords of ATs can change individual terms in an agreement; however, this procedure is not available to Rent Act landlords.

Tax considerations

Tax and financial matters are not considered in detail in this book and landlords are advised to seek professional advice from an accountant or refer to Lawpack's guide, *Tax Answers at a Glance*, where they can find a useful checklist of what they can claim against tax. Tax matters change annually and it is important that landlords are aware of the current regulations.

A landlord must inform HM Revenue & Customs that he is starting a rental business no later than 6 October after the end of the relevant tax year. Form SA1 should be used which can be downloaded from the HMRC website. As the HMRC can make random enquiries and/or specific enquiries of taxpayers at any time, it is essential that proper records are kept, as well as all invoices, receipts and bank statements.

CHAPTER 9

Problem tenants

Take action quickly

It is essential that all problems with tenants are dealt with quickly. If you ignore them, they will just get worse. It is also wise to avoid a confrontation with tenants. If they have a complaint, try to put it right immediately. If the complaint is unreasonable, negotiate with them.

A landlord says ...

'If a tenant is always complaining, he is usually working up to non-payment of rent.'

Landlord's duty to other tenants

A landlord is not generally liable for the acts of his tenants. But he may be held responsible if he deliberately introduces tenants he knows will be bad tenants into, say, a shared house. He may also be responsible to tenants for damage caused by disrepair in one of his other tenanted properties (e.g. from leaking pipes), for which he is responsible.

However, although a landlord cannot be held responsible for the acts of his bad tenants, he may feel that he owes a moral duty to his other tenants to take steps to evict the troublesome tenant, if only to prevent the other, good, tenants from leaving the property.

If you believe a tenant is going to visit his local Housing Advice Officer to complain, go down there yourself first and ask for advice about how to deal with your problems with the tenant. If you get your story in first and the Housing Officer sees that you are a reasonable person, he is less likely to write threatening letters to you.

Gas safety

Problems may occur when a tenant refuses access to a landlord to enable him to carry out the annual gas inspection. In the event of an incident, it will be for the landlord (or his managing agent) to show that he has taken all reasonable steps to meet his legal duties (and to avoid being prosecuted and fined). A suggested procedure is as follows:

- Tell the tenant when the inspection test will take place and give a telephone number to contact if this time is inconvenient, so another appointment can be arranged.

- If no communication is received from the tenant and the inspector is not able to gain access, write a letter to the tenant explaining that a gas safety check is a legal requirement and that it is for the tenant's own safety. Give the tenant an opportunity to make another appointment or suggest a further appointment.

- If after, say, 21 days the tenant still fails to contact you or allow access, send a further letter, reiterating the importance of the test and asking that the tenant contact you urgently to arrange an appointment within a specified period (say 14 days).

- You should not use force to gain access to the property.

- If, after three attempts, you are still unable to gain access in order to have the safety check done, contact your local Health & Safety Executive.

- Threats of violence from the tenant will justify cutting short this process.

Records (giving the date and time and any other details) should be kept of all visits to the property and copies should be kept of all correspondence sent to the tenant.

Tip

If a landlord thinks that any gas appliances are faulty and/or there is a gas escape, he should contact National Grid on 0800 111 999; it has statutory rights of entry and powers of disconnection.

Harassment legislation

It is beyond the scope of this book to consider harassment legislation in detail. Essentially, the legislation provides that harassment can be both a criminal offence and entitles the tenant to bring civil proceedings for an injunction (or interdict in Scotland) and/or damages.

- **Criminal prosecutions** are normally brought by local authorities after tenants have been to them to complain. They will always write to the landlord first, however, so any correspondence received from them should be treated seriously.

- **Civil proceedings** will be brought by the tenants themselves, usually with Legal Aid. They can prove extremely expensive for landlords, because if the tenant wins, the landlord will have to pay not only damages but also the tenant's legal costs.

The following are examples of actions which will entitle tenants and/or local authorities to invoke the legislation:

- Actual physical eviction of tenants from residential property by landlords. **Eviction of tenants should only ever be done by a court bailiff or High Court Sheriff (or Sheriff Officer in Scotland) pursuant to a court order.**

- Threats of, or actual, violence and/or verbal abuse.

- Removal of doors, windows and other items from the property.

- Disconnection of services, such as gas and electricity.

- Entering the property without the tenant's consent.

- Any act which is likely to cause the tenant to give up his occupancy of the property (even if this is not the landlord's intention).

Many landlords feel extremely frustrated by this legislation, when they see the tenants living in their property without paying rent, perhaps causing damage to the property, and using it for illegal purposes. However horrendous the tenant's conduct, though, the landlord must always follow the correct procedures and should **never** resort to self-help measures. There are legal remedies available to deal with tenants who behave badly, although unfortunately they do take some time. If a landlord does not follow the proper procedure, he can find it an extremely expensive exercise.

An example

A landlord lets a flat to a young lady. She only pays the first month's rent. She then starts behaving badly, she has loud parties and the neighbours complain. Her boyfriend causes a disturbance at the property on several occasions and kicks one of the doors in. The police are called in several times. The landlord goes round several times to ask for the rent. He tells her that unless she pays the rent and behaves properly she will have to go. On at least one occasion he loses his temper and shouts at her. One week he finds that she is not at the property. He continues to visit the property but she is never there. After about three weeks he suspects that she has left and uses his keys to gain entry. The house is in a dirty condition and it is obvious that no-one has been there for some time. It is full of rubbish and there is mouldy food in the kitchen. He finds some of her personal things, such as a purse with £5 in it, clothes in the wardrobe and in the chest of drawers in the bedroom, and some DVDs in the lounge. However, he decides that she has left, bags up all the items left in the property, and changes the locks. None of the items left being saleable, he dumps them (apart from the money in the purse which he takes against the rent arrears), redecorates the flat, and then relets it to another tenant.

Two months later he learns of a scene at the flat when the young lady tries to gain entry and is refused by the new tenant. He is subsequently served with a County court summons for damages for harassment and unlawful eviction together with a claim for compensation for her property, and a notice stating that she has been awarded Legal Aid. He loses the case and is ordered to pay compensation to the tenant, although the sum is reduced to take account of her unpaid rent and damage to the flat. He also has to pay her legal costs, which run into several thousand pounds, as well as his own solicitor's bill.

This landlord would also have been vulnerable to a prosecution for unlawful eviction.

Had the landlord followed the correct procedure and obtained a possession order, the tenant would not have been able to make any claim against him. He would have been out of pocket but the sums involved would have been far less.

Every landlord who lets property for any period of time is bound to have at least one bad tenant. All you can do is be careful in your choice of tenant, act swiftly to resolve any problems, and if the problem cannot be resolved, follow the correct legal procedures for evicting the tenant. Unfortunately, having the occasional bad tenant is just part of the job of being a landlord and when it happens to you, you just have to accept this and deal with it in a professional way.

A landlord says ...

'A tenant who is trouble at the beginning of a tenancy will continue to be trouble to the end.'

Evicting tenants

When evicting tenants, you need to have a 'ground' for eviction and to have served the proper notice on the tenant before legal proceedings are started.

Note

Unless specifically stated, this part of the book deals only with assured tenancies (ATs) under the Housing Act 1988 (this includes ASTs) and the Housing (Scotland) Act 1988. Any references to section numbers refer to sections in those Acts, as appropriate.

Grounds for possession

These are divided into mandatory grounds and discretionary grounds. It is strongly recommended that landlords only ever evict if they have mandatory grounds for possession, as this means that the judge has no alternative but to grant an order for possession. If only discretionary grounds are claimed, the tenant may be able to get Legal Aid to defend the proceedings and you will be faced with a large legal bill if you lose.

Also, if a possession order is granted under a discretionary ground the tenant has the right to ask the court to delay the actual possession date if he agrees to pay off any rent arrears by instalments, and the court will usually agree to this (even if you do not). However, under a mandatory ground, once the order is made, possession is normally ordered to be given up within 14 days, and the judge can only delay the date for possession for up to six weeks if the tenant can prove exceptional hardship.

There are several mandatory grounds for possession, but two that are most commonly used are:

- **The shorthold ground.** If a tenancy is an assured shorthold tenancy (AST) (or a short assured tenancy [SAT] in Scotland), the landlord is entitled to a possession order as of right, after the fixed term has expired, provided the proper form of notice (called a Section 21 notice) is served and all the preconditions have been met. In Scotland, a Section 33 notice is served along with a notice to quit, which must be in the correct statutory form.

- **Serious rent arrears (Ground 8).** Provided that both at the time of service of the notice (a Section 8 notice) and at the time of the court hearing, the tenant is in arrears of rent of more than eight weeks or two months, the landlord will be entitled to possession as of right. In Scotland, the landlord needs to serve a notice to quit and an AT6 notice specifying Ground 8 and the tenant must be in arrears of more than three months.

Tip

When claiming under Ground 8, it is normal to also quote Grounds 10 and 11 (any rent arrears and persistent late payment of rent). These are discretionary grounds relating to rent, but they will not normally be sufficient to obtain a possession order on their own. You can also use them when claiming under another ground (e.g. Ground 1) so you can get a money judgment for any rent arrears.

The owner-occupier ground, which allows owner-occupiers to recover possession of their homes, and which is another mandatory ground, is far less common now. This is because the shorthold ground is now generally used, and because the accelerated procedure (see below) cannot now be used for this ground.

There are other mandatory grounds, but these are rarely used and are not discussed in this book.

Most tenancies are shorthold nowadays, and if a tenant proves unsatisfactory, it is best simply to serve the Section 21 notice (or a Section 33 notice and a notice to quit in Scotland) and then issue proceedings under the shorthold ground at the end of the term. If the tenant's behaviour is so serious that you cannot wait, inform the police (if appropriate) and take legal advice immediately.

Possession notices

The shorthold ground – Section 21 notices

There has been considerable change recently regarding the interpretation of Section 21, and in England only, further changes came into force under the Deregulation Act 2015 on 1 October 2015. For landlords of property in Wales, the law will change radically with the Renting Homes (Wales) Bill, so they need to keep up to date with its progress; the changes in the Deregulation Act apply only to England. There are two forms of notice that can be served:

Under Section 21(1)(b), a notice must be in writing, must give the tenant not less than two months notice and must not end before the end of the fixed term (if it is served before the end of the fixed term).

Under Section 21(4)(a) the notice, which is intended to be served after the fixed term has ended, must in addition not give less notice to the tenant than they would be entitled to on a common law notice to quit and the notice must end 'after' the end of a period of the tenancy.

The Section 21(4) form of notice has caused great problems in the past, with landlords regularly failing to realise the importance of giving an expiry date which is the last day of a period of the tenancy. However, under the Court of Appeal decision of Spencer v. Taylor (approved by the Supreme Court) it was held that the easier form of notice, the Section 21(1)(b) notice can in addition be served during the periodic tenancy which follows the fixed term provided:

- there has been an initial fixed term and

- the periodic tenancy is a statutory periodic tenancy rather than a contractual one.

The Deregulation Act 2015 has also provided that for tenancies in England which are started or renewed on or after 1 October 2015 (and after 1 October 2018, all ASTs in England), it is not longer necessary to give a date which is the last day of a period of the tenancy.

So now you only need to use the more complex Section 21(4)(a) notice where there has never been an initial fixed term or if the periodic tenancy arises under contract (for example, because of a term in the tenancy agreement) rather than under statute (specifically Section 5 of the Housing Act 1988). Further, in England you will now only ever use the more complex section 21(4) notice (the one where you have to give the 'last day of a period of the tenancy') for section 21 notices created for the older, pre-1 October 2015 tenancies, and it will be phased out altogether in England after 1 October 2018.

Section 21 notices will also be invalid in any of the following scenarios:

- if the property is an HMO which requires licensing and the landlord has not obtained a licence;

- if a deposit has been taken, it has not been properly protected and the prescribed information not served, as discussed in chapter 7;

  additionally, for tenancies in England which started or were renewed on or after 1 October 2015:

- if an EPC has not been served on the tenants;

- if a gas safety certificate has not been served on the tenants;

- if the government's *How to Rent* booklet has not been served on the tenants (see chapter 6); and

- if one of the local authority notices (as discussed in the anti retaliatory eviction section in chapter 8) has been served on the tenant within the past six months.

Note that there is now a prescribed form of Section 21 notice. This needs to be served on all tenancies which started or were renewed on or after 1 October 2015 (and after 1 October 2018 will need to be served for all ASTs). Note that before this, it is not recommended that this notice be served for the older tenancies. The reason for this is that it sets out the new rules – which will not apply to the older tenancies and this may confuse tenants.

Time limits for Section 21 notices

In the past, section 21 notices have had an indefinite life and have only been ended if the tenancy ends – either after an order for possession has been made or by the landlord giving a new fixed term to the tenant.

However, for tenancies which are started or renewed on or after 1 October 2015 (and after 1 October 2018, all ASTs) there are now two new time limits.

1. The notice cannot be served during the first four months of a new tenancy (although if the tenancy is being renewed, this four month period will run from the start of the original fixed term).

2. There is now a time limit for using the section 21 notice. This is six months beginning on the date on which the notice was given. However, for periodic tenancies where the notice period required is more than two months, proceedings must start within four months of the date specified in the notice.

The shorthold ground – Scotland

In Scotland, the notice must be for at least two months prior to the end of the fixed term and a notice to quit in the prescribed statutory form must also be served at the same time. If no notices are served the tenancy continues by 'tacit relocation' for the term of the tenancy; so if the tenancy agreement is for six months, the tenancy will continue for a further period of six months and notices must be served at least two months before the end of the further six-month period.

Notices – other grounds

In England & Wales, the notice must be issued in the form prescribed by Section 8 of the Act, and if parts of it are missing or crossed out in error, it may be invalid. If you are serving the notice under Ground 1, it will need to be a two-month notice, if you are serving notice under Ground 8, it is a two-week notice. Note this prescribed form was amended from 6 April 2015, and using the old form could invalidate any court proceedings based on it. There is also a slight amendment to notices served on AST tenants whose tenancies were started or renewed after 1 October 2015.

In Scotland, Form AT6 is served for the period prescribed by the Housing (Scotland) Act 1988. To terminate the tenancy you must also serve a notice to quit, which has a notice period of at least 40 days; for example, even if you serve an AT6 under Ground 8, which is a two-week notice, you still need to serve a notice to quit with 40 days' notice.

General advice on notices

If you are not sure what you are doing, you should get a solicitor to draft the notice for you. It is essential that the notice is correct as otherwise you may not be granted a possession order at court. Sometimes what appear to be quite minor inaccuracies can prove fatal at court.

If you are intending to bring proceedings for possession based on rent arrears, the deposit regulations will be important. If you have failed to protect or serve the prescribed information, you will have no defence to a claim for the penalty payment. The effect of this will be to offset and therefore effectively reduce the rent due to you and could cancel it out altogether.

Always keep a copy of the notice served and a record of the date and time of service of the notice, the method of service (by post, personally, or through the letter box) and the name of the person who served it. It is recommended that notices are served either by handing them to the tenant personally (the best method of service) or by putting them (in an envelope addressed to the tenant) through the letter box of the property yourself. In Scotland the notices are required to be served either by recorded delivery or sheriff officer. If time is short it might be better to have the notices served by sheriff officer as the tenant may refuse to sign for the recorded delivery letter.

Tip

If you think that your tenant will lie and say that you did not serve the notice, have an independent witness with you.

I recommend that you do not send them by post, as it is all too easy for the tenant to say that they got lost in the post. If this happens after you have issued proceedings, there is no way that you can prove delivery by the post office, so you will have to cancel those proceedings and start again.

However, if you have written proof of receipt from the tenants (e.g. if they have referred to the notice in a letter) you should be safe. I prefer not to use recorded delivery as the tenant can refuse to accept delivery, which can cause problems.

Possession proceedings

For ATs and ASTs, there are two types of possession proceedings you can use, the 'normal' proceedings and the (so called) 'accelerated' proceedings.

- **Accelerated proceedings.** These can only be used if your ground for possession is the shorthold ground. It cannot be used to claim rent arrears. It is quicker because the evidence is given by way of a written statement to the court and there is no court hearing. If successful, you will get an order for possession (normally enforceable 14 days after the order was made) and an order that the tenant pay 'fixed costs' (if you are acting in person, this will just be the court fee). From the issue of proceedings to receipt of the order for possession, these proceedings normally take between six and ten weeks assuming nothing goes wrong.

- **Normal 'fixed date' proceedings.** These involve a court hearing where you will have to attend and present your case to the judge. However, you will also normally be entitled to a money judgment for any rent arrears due at the date of the hearing, and an order that the tenant pays future rent until he vacates the property. If the rent arrears remain unpaid, you can enforce this judgment through the courts. You will also be entitled to an order for costs (if you are acting in person, this will normally be limited to the court fee and your costs of attending the hearing). In Scotland, all proceedings for possession are under the 'summary cause procedure' at the Sheriff Court, unless in addition you are seeking payment of rent arrears in excess of £5000, in which case an ordinary action should be raised. In all cases under the summary cause procedure, a hearing is fixed.

Unless you are very certain of what you are doing, it is really best to instruct a solicitor should it become necessary to evict your tenant. Judges do not like making possession orders and will usually refuse to do so, unless a landlord has got his paperwork right. If you make a mistake, a tenant will be able to defend (often with Legal Aid) and you may end up with no possession order and an order to pay the tenant's legal costs.

Acting in person

If you do not want to use a solicitor, you will have to act in person and bring the proceedings yourself. Note that the court papers can only be signed by either the landlord himself or his solicitor. A letting agent cannot sign on behalf of a landlord. The court will also need to have an address for service for the claimant (i.e. the person bringing the proceedings) in England & Wales, so landlords living abroad will need to instruct solicitors to act for them.

If you decide to act in person, you will find all the necessary forms and some helpful leaflets on the Court Service website at http://goo.gl/PwyGJl (or www.scotcourts.gov.uk for Scotland). They are also available from the Court Office of your local County court in England & Wales or the Sheriff Clerk's Office or local Sheriff Court in Scotland. Fill in the forms as indicated, and make sure that when you issue the proceedings you send a cheque for the court fee (currently £280) made payable to HM Courts and Tribunals Service or HMCTS and an extra copy of the form and any attached documents, for each defendant. In Scotland, the current fee under the summary cause procedure is £65 and cheques should be made payable to the Scottish Courts Administration.

Note that you can now issue some types of possession proceedings online via the court service website at www.possessionclaim.gov.uk/pcol. If you use this service there is a lower court fee.

Tip

Make sure that you do not issue proceedings until after your possession notice has expired, or the claim will be invalid.

The court will issue the proceedings and serve a copy on each defendant. At the same time you will be informed of this by notice. If you are issuing normal proceedings, you will be told the date of the court hearing (in Scotland, a hearing is always fixed in summary cause proceedings); if you are using the accelerated procedure, you will be told when you can apply to the court for a possession order. If the defendant files a defence or response to your proceedings, you should be sent a copy by the court (although it is sometimes rather slow in doing this). In Scotland, you require to serve the action on the defender. The court will fix two dates, the return date which is the latest date when the defender can advise the court he is defending the proceedings and also a hearing date when the landlord or his solicitor is required to attend to ask the sheriff to grant the decree of eviction (and a decree for rent arrears if applicable). Once the action has been raised against the tenant, the landlord or his solicitor has to serve a notice on the local authority. If the action is defended a full hearing called a 'proof' will be fixed at which both sides will be required to call witnesses and produce documentary evidence. In Scotland, the defender has to lodge his written defence with the court and at the same time provide his landlord with a copy.

Read carefully all communications you receive from the court and follow any instructions given to you. If you need to contact the court about the case, it is essential that you quote the case number, as otherwise the court staff will not be able to locate the proper file or deal with your enquiry. Remember that it takes the court some time to deal with the issue of proceedings and enquiries; do not expect a response too soon. Some courts are slower than others, in particular London courts, being very busy.

Tip

Many courts are now so busy that it is very difficult to speak to staff on the phone. It may be easier to send an email to the court - normally you will get a reply within two days (depending again on how busy the court is).

If you are using the normal proceedings or if a hearing is listed for any other type of claim (e.g. if a defence is filed in a claim brought by the accelerated procedure), make sure that you arrive at court in good time (if you are late, the case may be heard without you and your claim dismissed). If you are unavoidably detained, for example if you get stuck in traffic or have an accident, try to contact the court and let it know when you will be arriving. It may then be able to delay hearing the case until you arrive. When you arrive at court you should look at the lists for that day, which you will find pinned to a notice board, usually near the entrance. This will tell you in which court your case is being heard and the name of the judge. You should then go to the court room and (this is most important) tell the usher you have arrived. He will then make sure that you are told when the case is being heard. If you do not contact the usher, no-one will know that you are there and, again, there is a possibility that the case may be heard without you.

Standard proceedings are normally listed at half-hour intervals and several cases will be listed together. However, if you are near the end of the list, it may be some time before your case is called, so do not expect to be called immediately (in the author's experience the only times a case is called on at the time listed is when you are late). If you are in a car park where you have to pay in advance, do make sure that you pay enough to cover any delays. Note that if several of the cases in the list take longer than expected, cases further down may find that they are being called up to an hour or even two hours late.

Most possession proceedings and applications are now heard 'in chambers', which means that they are heard in the judge's private room and not in an open court (in Scotland where they are heard in open court). The judges are District Judges and you should address them as 'Sir' or 'Ma'am' (not 'Your Honour'). In Scotland, the proceedings are held in open court and the judge is the Sheriff and should be addressed as 'Your Lordship' or 'M'Lord' or 'Your Ladyship' or 'M'Lady'.

The claimant is heard first and will have to state his case and give evidence to support his claim. For example, for a rent arrears claim, you will have to tell the court the current rent arrears. The judge will then ask the defendant (if he attends the hearing) some questions and give him an opportunity to give his case. The judge will then make his decision. He sometimes makes a little speech when doing this and if so, it is important that you make a note of what he says (in case you disagree with it and want to take legal advice later). If the judge finds in your favour, you can then ask for your costs which, if you are acting in person, will just be the court fee and your expenses for attending the hearing. If the defendant does not attend (and defendants frequently fail to attend), you will still have to give your evidence, but it is more likely that you will succeed in getting the order that you want.

After the hearing you will be sent a court order confirming what was decided by the judge. Do check this carefully as occasionally there are mistakes. If there is an error, write to the court and ask it to amend the errors.

Note – there is a series of posts on the author's website www.landlordlawblog.co.uk called the 'Novice Guide to Court Hearings', which will be helpful if you are representing yourself.

Instructing a solicitor

If you decide to instruct a solicitor, make sure he is one who is experienced in this type of work (many are not), and that you get a firm quotation for his costs before he does any work. Make sure that this quotation is confirmed in writing. For straightforward possession claims the solicitor should be able to quote you a fixed fee. The solicitor will need:

- The tenancy agreement.
- Copies of all notices served on the tenant.
- Details of how, when, and by whom the notices were served.
- Confirmation that all the preconditions have been complied with.
- Any correspondence with the tenant, and any other notes and paperwork.
- Confirmation that the tenancy deposit (if you took one) has been protected with a government-authorised tenancy deposit scheme, been properly registered and the notice served on the tenant.
- A schedule of the rent arrears (if you are claiming unpaid rent).
- A payment on account of costs.

Tip

Make sure that the property is in good repair before issuing proceedings for serious rent arrears. If it is not, the tenant will be able to bring a counterclaim against you (often with the benefit of Legal Aid) which may prevent you from getting possession and also make you liable for an award of damages and an order to pay his legal costs.

Evicting Rent Act tenants

It is beyond the scope of this book to deal with the eviction of Rent Act tenants. If you wish to evict a Rent Act tenant, you should seek specialist legal advice. Generally, however, you are only likely to succeed if the tenant is in serious arrears of rent, or if you are able to offer him suitable alternative accommodation.

Common law tenancies

There are some tenancies which are not covered by either the Rent Act 1997 or the Housing Act 1988. These are generally tenancies of self-contained accommodation in the property where the owner himself lives, properties let at a high rent (currently more than £100,000 per annum) or at a low rent (£1,000 per annum in Greater London or £250 per annum elsewhere), and company lets. For these tenancies you will need to serve an old-style notice to quit and then issue the standard proceedings (with a court hearing). As this type of procedure is non-standard, it is probably best to take advice from a housing solicitor before taking any action. However, if these claims are drafted and issued correctly, they can be less problematic than claims for possession for AT and AST tenancies.

Squatters and licensees

If the person occupying the property does not have a tenancy, then you will be able to use another form of possession proceedings. These proceedings are much quicker than those used for tenancies and you can sometimes obtain a possession order in less than two weeks. In Scotland, you do not need to serve notices, but the court procedure can still take about two months.

However, it is not advisable for a landlord to bring this type of proceeding on his own unless he really knows what he is doing. It would be much better to instruct a reliable firm of solicitors, experienced in eviction work.

Note that if a squatter has entered a property by breaking in, or if there is someone living at the property (known as a 'displaced occupier') the police should help you gain possession of the property and it should not be necessary for you to go to court. The police were given new powers to deal with squatters in residential premises under section 144 of the Legal Aid, Sentencing and Punishing of Offenders Act 2012. However, it remains to be seen how often these powers will actually be used in practice.

Note

A tenant cannot become a squatter simply by staying on in the property after the end of his fixed term. He will still be a tenant.

Enforcement of possession orders

Even if you have a possession order, you cannot enforce this other than through the court bailiff or High Court Sheriff(or Sheriff Officer in Scotland). Do not physically evict the tenant (or occupiers) yourself! If you do, this will be a criminal offence.

The possession order (or Court Decree in Scotland) will give a date for possession. Unless specifically authorised by the court, you will have to wait until after this date before instructing the bailiffs (or Sheriff Officer in Scotland). If the tenant is still in the property at that time, you will have to complete a request form and send this, together with the court fee, to court (or you may be able to issue via the court online procedure). It will normally take some weeks for an appointment to be arranged (unless you are evicting squatters, when the bailiffs usually act quickly). The bailiff usually visits the property before fixing the appointment to discuss the eviction with the occupiers.

In Scotland, once you have the Court Decree you can instruct the Sheriff Officer to serve it on the tenant and if he has not vacated by the date given by the Sheriff Officer the Sheriff Officer can evict him. There is no need to go back to court. When an appointment is made, you must always arrange for someone to attend with the bailiff and formally take possession from him. You should also arrange for a locksmith to be present to change the locks. In Scotland, a Sheriff Officer will attend to this as long as you instruct him to do so.

For evictions in England and Wales which need to be done quickly or where you anticipate problems from the tenants, there is a quicker (although more expensive) service available via the High Court Sheriffs. You need to get leave of the court first however before using this. For more information see www.sherbond.net.

Excluded tenancies or licences

If the letting is (a) to a lodger in your own home where you share living accommodation with the lodger, or (b) a holiday let, there is no duty on you, in most cases, to obtain an order for possession for the purposes of criminal law. You must, however, tell the occupier in writing that you want him to leave and give the occupier a reasonable period of time to vacate. However, if it is clear that the tenant is not going to vacate voluntarily, you should consult a solicitor. You may still have to issue possession proceedings, for example of the type discussed above for squatters and licensees.

Money claims

There may be times when landlords wish to claim for rent, but do not want or need to claim for possession, for example if the tenant has already left the property, or if the tenant (or Housing Benefit) is paying rent but there are a few weeks' rent outstanding, perhaps relating to the period before Housing Benefit started. Also, the landlord will have a claim against the tenant if he has vacated the property leaving it in a poor condition, and the damage deposit is insufficient to cover the landlord's costs of putting things right. This type of claim is known as a claim for 'dilapidations'.

Many landlords are also defendants in proceedings brought by tenants for the return of their damage deposit where there is a dispute about the landlords' entitlement to retain them or will be involved in arbitration under the new tenancy deposit protection schemes if there is a dispute regarding the payment of the deposit. However, for information about damage deposits please see chapter 7.

Money claims should be brought in the County court and, if (as is usual) they are for sums of less than £5,000, they will be dealt with by the small claims procedure. It is also possible to issue proceedings online at Money Claim Online via the court website at www.moneyclaim.gov.uk.

In Scotland, claims should be brought to the Sheriff Court; sums of up to £3,000 are dealt with under the small claims procedure. Sums of £3,000 to £5,000 can be dealt with by summary cause procedure. Sums above £5,000 are dealt with under ordinary procedure.

When bringing proceedings against tenants, landlords should ensure that they have evidence to support each and every element of their claim. For claiming rent arrears they will need a detailed rent statement showing how the rent arrears accrued. Claims for interest should be kept entirely separate and should not be included in this schedule. For claims for damages, landlords will need either an estimate or an invoice for the cost of all items/work claimed. If witnesses are to be used, you will need to have a written statement of what they are going to say, which should be signed and dated. They will, however, usually still need to attend the hearing. You will also need to prepare a written statement of your own evidence.

If the claim is defended and goes to a hearing, both sides will be ordered by the judge to produce (so far as is possible) and serve on each other, all relevant documents. These will probably include:

- the tenancy agreement;
- the inventory;
- evidence of rent payments (e.g. the rent book)
- any witness statements;
- invoices or estimates for work and goods; and
- a schedule setting out the items that are being claimed giving details of the sums claimed.

You will need to take the original documents with you to the hearing.

Notes on dilapidations claims

Claims for rent arrears should be fairly straightforward – the tenant has either paid the rent or not. However, claims for dilapidations can be more complex. Below are some points for landlords to bear in mind when bringing this type of claim:

- If the damage done by the tenant exceeds the amount of the damage deposit, then, if the deposit is protected under one of the tenancy deposit protection schemes, you will have to bring a separate claim in the County court for the additional amount.

- This is really only worth doing if there is a realistic chance of the tenants actually being able to pay any judgment made in your favour; for example, it is seldom worth the effort of bringing a claim against housing benefit tenants (unless they subsequently get a job) and you may prefer just to look to your insurance to cover your loss.

- If you decide to bring a claim, you will have to prove that the damage was actually done by the tenant; for example, the tenant may seek to claim that the damage was already done before he moved in or was done after he vacated.

- If there is a detailed signed inventory, the tenant will find it difficult to prove that the damage was done before he moved in. However, you should take care to do your final inventory check at the time or immediately after the tenant vacates, so your tenant cannot claim that the damage was done after he left.

- Note you cannot claim for damage occasioned by 'fair wear and tear.'

- One advantage of having the inventory, and the check-in and check-out meetings done by an independent inventory company is that they will be seen by the court as an impartial witness.

- There is a technical rule (in Section 18(1) of the Landlord and Tenant Act 1927) which says that a landlord cannot claim more than the diminution caused to his reversion (i.e. the value of the property when he regains possession) by the state of the premises at the end of the tenancy. So, if the property should have been worth £100,000 when you got it back, but due to the damage to the property done by the tenants it is actually worth £70,000, you will not be entitled to claim more than £30,000 from the tenants. Note that the rule does not include damage to the property contents, just to the property itself.

- If the landlord has had repair work done, the court will normally accept the invoices as being evidence of the value of the damage to the landlord's reversion, provided it was reasonable for him to do the work and the sums charged were reasonable.

- However, if you have not had any repair work done, you may have difficulty proving your case. If you have no invoices or estimates for the proposed work, the court may dismiss your claim. Make sure therefore that you have paperwork to prove every item you are claiming.

- Sometimes you may also want to claim for rent lost as a result of having to carry out the repair work. However, to claim this you will have to establish how long it would reasonably have taken you to let the property if it had been in a proper condition, and then show that the works done extended this period.

- The tenant may be entitled to ask the court to reduce any sum awarded to you reflect 'betterment' i.e. the fact that after the works are done you will be getting back a property in a better condition than you were entitled to expect.

CHAPTER 10

At the end of a tenancy

When does the tenancy end?

In practice, in one of the following situations:

1. at the end of the term when the tenant leaves voluntarily;

2. when the tenant vacates after service of a notice to terminate (served by either the landlord or the tenant);

3. by agreement with the landlord; or

4. when an order for possession has been made by the court.

Normally the tenant leaves voluntarily – to use legal terminology, he 'surrenders' the tenancy. A tenant cannot force the landlord to accept a surrender before the end of the term. However, landlords are advised to agree to release the tenant if there is another suitable tenant available to take over the tenancy, provided his reasonable expenses are paid. If the tenant leaves mid-way through the term, you can still claim rent from him and if he does not pay, obtain a County court judgment (or Sheriff Court Decree in Scotland) (provided you have his new address or a contact address). You will not be able to claim rent from him after you have relet the property to another tenant (apart from existing arrears).

Tip

Do not agree to accept a 'surrender' of a tenancy until any lodgers or other occupiers who are not tenants have vacated. Or make your acceptance conditional upon receiving vacant possession. Otherwise you may become bound by any agreement they had with your tenant and it will be more difficult for you to get him out.

Sometimes a tenant will just abandon a property without giving any notice. However, problems can arise when it is not certain whether a tenant has left or not. Obviously a landlord will want to relet a property as soon as possible, particularly if there are rent arrears. But a landlord must be extremely careful in these circumstances when re-entering the property, as he may be vulnerable to a charge of unlawful eviction.

You will usually be safe to repossess if:

- the fixed term has come to an end; and

- **all** the tenant's possessions have gone; and

- particularly if the keys have been returned to you or are left at the property.

Be very careful if the tenant has left items at the property, particularly if the term has not come to an end. The tenant may be on a long holiday, or be in hospital, or prison. If it is not absolutely clear that the tenant has vacated permanently, you should keep out of the property and obtain a possession order through the courts. See chapter 9.

Obviously you should only be considering re-entering and repossessing if the rent is in arrears. If the rent is paid up, you should not, except in the case of emergency, enter the property at all without the tenant's permission.

Be aware also that it is not unknown for tenants deliberately to entice a landlord into taking possession of a property by making it appear as if they have vacated, so that they can then bring a claim for damages for unlawful eviction.

Note – some landlords and agents rely on 'abandonment notices' pinned to the door, to excuse them from any need to bring proceedings for possession. Be aware that these have no real foundation in law and will only afford a very limited, if any, protection to any claim that a tenant may subsequently make for unlawful eviction. Such a notice may also attract the unwelcome attention of professional squatters.

Tip

If a tenant hands you his keys before the term has ended saying he wants to give up his tenancy, make it very clear that you do not accept his surrender, and that you will hold him responsible for the rent until another tenant is found. If you do not do this, you may be deemed to have accepted the surrender.

Handover procedure

When it is time for the tenant to go, you should arrange for an appointment with him at the property. You should then check over the contents and condition of the property with him, using the inventory and schedule of condition. Usually you should be able to decide there and then whether you will need to make any retention from the damage deposit and if so, how much this should be for. The damage deposit should then be returned to the tenant as soon as possible; or, if it is held by the custodial scheme administrators, they should be asked to release it, however, not until after:

- the tenants have vacated the property and returned the keys; and
- you are sure that there is not going to be any claw-back from the Housing Benefit Office.

Remember, when making retentions from the damage deposit, that you must allow for fair wear and tear. The property will normally have been occupied for a long period and it is unrealistic to expect it to be in the same pristine condition that it was, at the start of the tenancy. If it is left in a dirty condition, you are entitled to claim for the reasonable costs of having the property cleaned.

Tenants often complain that landlords seek to make deductions for damage done to the property when the damage should have come under the 'fair wear and tear' exception, and there is often some confusion as to when this should apply. An example:

- If a property is let with a rather worn carpet in the hall, and during the period of the tenancy someone's foot catches on a worn patch and it tears, this damage will come under the 'fair wear and tear' exception.

- However, if the property is provided with a brand new carpet at the start of the tenancy but when the tenant leaves this is found to have a number of cuts in it and/or large and unsightly stains which cannot be removed, then the tenant will normally be liable for the cost of a replacement carpet and the cost of this can be deducted from the damage deposit.

Make sure that you keep full records to back up any deductions made from damage deposits, for example estimates and receipts, photographs and (in bad cases) even a video to provide a record of the condition of the property after the tenant has left. Then if the tenant challenges any deductions made by you either via the tenancy deposit scheme arbitration service or (where the schemes do not apply) by bringing a County court claim for recovery of the damage deposit, you will have a good chance of defeating the claim. You should retain this information for at least six years.

Where the deposit is not protected under one of the statutory schemes, the deposit should be dealt with in the following way:

1. make deductions for damage/repairs/cleaning as appropriate; if any money is left, then

2. credit the balance against the rent arrears.

So, if there is a damage deposit of £500, damages to the value of £300 and rent arrears of £600, the £300 damages are taken first from the damage deposit leaving £200 to offset against the arrears. If you are then in a position to bring a County court claim against the tenant (i.e. if you have his new address and consider he will be worth suing), your claim will be for the balance of the rent arrears due, i.e. £400.

If the deposit is being held under one of the statutory schemes, you need to refer to the scheme's rules. For more information on the schemes, see chapter 7.

Tip

Do not return the damage deposit or agree to the release of the deposit to the tenant by the custodial scheme administrators until after you have done a careful inspection of the property – once you have returned the damage deposit it is very difficult, if not impossible, to get it back.

A letting agent says ...

'We find that most problems with damage deposits are caused by landlords being unreasonable about damage due to wear and tear.'

Tenant's property left behind

This is often a great problem for landlords, because they will want to clear the property and relet it as soon as possible. But landlords must be very careful when dealing with things left behind, particularly if the rented property was abandoned by the tenant, as it is not unknown for tenants to subsequently bring a claim for damages for the alleged valuable items destroyed (the author has experience of a case where Legal Aid was granted to the claimant in similar circumstances). Remember that unless the tenant has specifically given you permission to dispose of these items, you do not have the legal right to either sell them or dump them, as they do not belong to you. However, you can move them out of the property and store them elsewhere if necessary.

The procedure for dealing with this situation is laid down in an Act called the Torts (Interference with Goods) Act 1977 (not applicable in Scotland). Under this Act, a landlord can dispose of goods left behind as follows:

1. If the landlord sends a letter by recorded delivery to the tenant stating that he intends to sell/dispose of the goods and gives the following information:

    *   the name and address of the landlord (i.e. where he can be contacted regarding their collection); and

    *   details of the items held;

    *   the place where they are held; and

    *   the date after which he intends to sell the goods (this must give

the tenant a reasonable time to collect the goods - say two to four weeks).

Make sure you keep a copy of the letter sent, and the recorded delivery slip. If you are worried that the tenant will not accept the recorded delivery, it might also be an idea to hand deliver a copy of the letter to his address, so he cannot later claim that he has not received it.

2.   If the landlord does not have any address for the tenant, he can sell or dispose of the goods if he is able to show that he has made reasonable attempts to locate him. This is best done by instructing tracing agents. Many will offer a 'no-trace-no-fee' arrangement. Provided the tracing agent's report stating that he cannot locate the tenant is kept, the landlord should be safe from a claim from the tenant if he then sells or disposes of the goods.

When disposing of the goods, it is wise to keep a record of what has been done. If there is any possibility that the tenant could bring a claim, try to get an independent witness to make a statement about the items and their condition. If the goods have any value, they should be sold at the best price obtainable. Keep full records of what was done and the prices obtained.

If any of the goods are sold, the proceedings of sale are strictly speaking the property of the tenant and should be kept for him. However, the landlord is entitled to deduct the costs of sale, and if there are rent arrears outstanding or other monies due to the landlord, there is no reason why these should not also be deducted.

Death of a tenant

What happens if an assured tenancy or an assured shorthold tenancy tenant dies? If he is one of joint tenants, the tenancy will simply continue in the name of the other joint tenant/s. If the tenant is a sole tenant, then, as discussed in chapter 1, the tenancy will normally pass to the tenant's spouse or to a member of his family. If the tenancy passes to anyone other than the tenant's spouse, then the landlord has a mandatory ground for possession, provided proceedings are issued within 12 months of the tenant's death.

If the tenancy is a Rent Act tenancy, then the tenancy will pass as above to the spouse, family member, etc. The succession rights of tenants are stronger under Rent Act tenancies and there is no mandatory ground for possession.

It is beyond the scope of this book to consider the succession rights of tenants in detail. Landlords are advised to seek further advice from a solicitor, particularly if the tenant is a Rent Act tenant.

Note

If you need to serve a possession notice but you do not know who to serve it on, guidance can be obtained from the Official Solicitor, who has a website at http://www.justice.gov.uk/about/ospt.

For the position in Scotland, seek advice from a solicitor.

After the tenant has gone

Utilities

Make sure that a meter reading is done before the property is relet.

Post

If you do not have a forwarding address for the old tenant, do not keep or throw post away; return everything, marked 'gone away'.

You will then have to clean the property, redecorate it if necessary, and start all over again!

Tip

Try to obtain a forwarding address for the tenants. You may need it later if you have a claim against them.

Useful addresses

Association of Residential Letting Agents (ARLA)

ARLA Administration
Arbon House
6 Tournament Court
Edgehill
Warwick CV34 6LG

Tel: 0845 250 6001
Website: www.arla.co.uk

Clerk to the Rent Assessment Committee – Scotland

Sixth Floor
78 St Vincent Street
Glasgow G2 5UB

Tel: 0141 204 2261
Website: www.scotland.gov.uk

or

48 Manor Place
Edinburgh EH3 7EH

Tel: 0131 226 1123

Companies House

Crown Way
Maindy
Cardiff CF14 3UZ

Tel: 0303 1234 500
Website: www.companieshouse.
gov.uk

Competition and Markets Authority (formerly Office of Fair Trading)

Victoria House	Tel: 020 3738 6000
37 Southampton Row	Website: www..gov.uk
London WC1B 4AD	

Gas Safe Register

PO Box Basingstoke	Tel: 0800 408 5500
RG24 4NB	Website: www.gassaferegister.co.uk

If you smell gas then call the free
24-hour National Grid
Emergency Helpline:

England, Scotland and Wales:	0800 111 999
Northern Ireland:	0800 002 001
Jersey:	01534 755 555
Guernsey:	01481 749 000

Health & Safety Executive

HSE Infoline: 0845 345 0055   Website: www.hse.gov.uk

HM Revenue & Customs Stamp Duty Land Tax Helpline

Tel: 0845 603 0135   Website: www.hmrc.gov.uk/so

Housing Ombudsman

81 Aldwych	Tel: 0300 111 3000
London WC2B 4HN	Website: www.housing-ombudsman.org.uk

National Inspection Council for Electrical Installation Contracting (NICEIC)

Warwick House	Tel: 0870 013 0382
Houghton Hall Park	Website: www.niceic.org.uk
Houghton Regis	
Dunstable	
Bedfordshire LU5 5ZX	

National Landlords Association

2nd Floor, 200 Union Street London SE1 0LX	Tel: 020 7840 8900 Website: www.landlords.org.uk

Parliamentary and Health Service Ombudsman

Millbank Tower Millbank London SW1P 4QP	Tel: 0845 015 4033 Website: www.ombudsman. org.uk

Private Rented Housing Panel – Scotland

Europa Building 450 Argyle Street Glasgow G2 8LH	Tel: 0141 242 0142 Fax: 0141 242 0141 Website: www.prhpscotland.gov.uk

Royal Institution of Chartered Surveyors (RICS)

Parliament Square London SW1P 3AD	Tel: 024 7686 8555 Website: www.rics.org

Scottish Association of Landlords

Hopetoun Gate 8b McDonald Road Edinburgh EH7 4LZ	Tel: 0131 564 0100 Website: www.scottishlandlords.com

Index